'Puberty is a crucial time in a young person's life. Preparing children for puberty is different from talking with small children about where babies come from. Fortunately, this book supports you during this phase of young people's lives. *Going Beyond "The Talk"* shows you how to have honest and open conversations about sex and sexuality at home and in school. It gives relevant facts and advice to overcome your embarrassment to talk about the most intimate and sensitive issues around sex. I highly recommend it!'

– Doortje Braeken, former senior adviser of adolescents, gender and rights of the International Planned Parenthood Federation and international consultant for UNESCO, Plan International, Global Advisory Board for Sexual Health and Wellbeing

'The life raft that helps you navigate the choppy seas of sex(uality) education for adolescents and how to talk to them about it. Thank you for giving me the understanding, insight and tools to provide the right support. I only wish my parents had read it!'

– John Pope CBE

'This warm, hopeful, evidence-based guide is filled with wisdom and has inclusivity at its heart. It is a must-read for all adults wishing to communicate with their teenagers about relationships, sexuality, identity and values like never before. It will challenge you and affirm you in equal measure.'

– Katy Thomas, relationships and sexuality education researcher, teacher, mother of four

'This book is an eminently readable resource for anyone caring for a teenager. It gives a very clear picture of teenage development, which helps us to understand our own biases and how to overcome these so that our teenagers get the love, support and understanding they need.'

– Arushi Singh, UN specialist on sexuality education

'A highly engaging book exploring relationships, consent, respect, sexuality and identity in an accessible way. It brings together the informal learning of the home and the formal learning of schooling to provide a coherent, inclusive and joined-up approach to young people's development.'
– Professor Richard Woolley, University of Hull

'This is a unique book which successfully unifies sexuality education in school and at home. It is a practical tool for an intergenerational dialogue and addressing serious questions raised by young people. The parents and educators will find here the right words and approaches to support young people in staying safe and achieving well-being. But most of all, the reader of this book will feel the joy of sexuality education classes.'
– Drashko Kostovski, IPPF European Network

Going Beyond 'The Talk'

by the same authors

Can I Have Babies Too?
Sexuality and Relationships Education for Children from Infancy up to Age 11
Sanderijn van der Doef, Clare Bennett and Arris Lueks
ISBN 978 1 78775 500 0
eISBN 978 1 78775 501 7

of related interest

Creating Consent Culture
A Handbook for Educators
Marcia Baczynski and Erica Scott
ISBN 978 1 83997 102 0
eISBN 978 1 83997 103 7

The Every Body Book
The LGBTQ+ Inclusive Guide for Kids about Sex, Gender, Bodies, and Families
Rachel E. Simon, LCSW
Illustrated by Noah Grigni
ISBN 978 1 78775 173 6
eISBN 978 1 78775 174 3

What Does Consent Really Mean?
Pete Wallis and Thalia Wallis
Illustrated by Joseph Wilkins
ISBN 978 1 84819 330 7
eISBN 978 0 85701 285 2

We Need to Talk about Pornography
A Resource to Educate Young People about the Potential Impact of Pornography
and Sexualised Images on Relationships, Body Image and Self-Esteem
Vanessa Rogers
ISBN 978 1 84905 620 5
eISBN 978 1 78450 091 7

Going Beyond 'The Talk'

RELATIONSHIPS AND SEXUALITY
EDUCATION FOR THOSE
SUPPORTING 12–18 YEAR OLDS

Sanderijn van der Doef, Clare Bennett and Arris Lueks

ILLUSTRATED BY MARIAN LATOUR

Jessica Kingsley Publishers
London and Philadelphia

First published in Great Britain in 2022 by Jessica Kingsley Publishers
An imprint of Hodder & Stoughton Ltd
An Hachette Company

2

A CIP catalogue record for this title is available from the
British Library and the Library of Congress

ISBN 978 1 78775 512 3
eISBN 978 1 78775 513 0

Printed and bound in the United States by Integrated Books International

Jessica Kingsley Publishers' policy is to use papers that are natural,
renewable and recyclable products and made from wood grown in sus-
tainable forests. The logging and manufacturing processes are expected to
conform to the environmental regulations of the country of origin.

Jessica Kingsley Publishers
Carmelite House
50 Victoria Embankment
London EC4Y 0DZ

www.jkp.com

To our pre-teen children, teenagers and grown up children who have taught us so much about life. We hope that this book makes a small contribution to making the world a more compassionate place for you to grow up and thrive in.

Voor onze eigen pubers, bijna pubers en volwassen pubers, die ons zoveel over het leven hebben geleerd. We hopen van harte dat we met dit boek een beetje hebben kunnen bijgedragen aan een meer begripvolle wereld waarin jullie kunnen opgroeien en gedijen.

Contents

Acknowledgements

Without the help and generosity of many colleagues, parents, carers and young people around the world, this book wouldn't be the comprehensive resource it has become. We are extremely grateful to you all.

We wish to thank a number of experts who have helped to shape the book to ensure that it is contemporary and relevant to young people's lives internationally. We are particularly grateful to Susie Jolly, Honorary Associate at the Institute of Development Studies and independent consultant, researcher and facilitator; thank you for your valuable comments and ideas, especially about gender and gender equality. Likewise, Doortje Braeken, international expert in sexual reproductive health and rights of young people, former colleague and long-time friend, has been incredibly generous in going through the text from beginning to end; her suggestions have significantly improved the content of the book and we are very grateful to her. Thank you too to Sensoa, and especially Erika Frans, for allowing us to describe and helping us apply the Sensoa Flag System to adolescent development.

A huge thank you must also go to the Winston Churchill Memorial Trust and Cardiff University's Erasmus+ Organisational Mobility for funding the original projects from which our first book *Can I Have Babies Too?* and this book evolved. Thank you too to Peter Oates of Lantern Press for helping us find a publisher for these books and to James Cherry for supporting us in securing a contract for publication.

We also wish to extend our gratitude to the parents, carers, grandparents, teachers and other professionals across the world who contributed to this book by telling us about their needs and those of the adolescents in their lives with regards to relationships and sexuality education. And of course, last but certainly not least, a big thank you to all the adolescents who shared their needs and thoughts with us about how they would like to be educated about relationships and sexuality.

We hope that this book inspires our readers as much as all of you wonderful people have inspired us!

Sanderijn, Clare and Arris

Introduction

GROWING UP IN THE 21ST CENTURY: FROM MADONNA'S 'LIKE A VIRGIN' (1984) TO CARDI B AND MEGAN THEE STALLION'S 'WAP' (2020)

Did you grow up with Madonna's 'Like a Virgin'? Or another song/group? Who did you adore or want to be like? What was cool? What hairstyle did you have or want? And... how did you feel?

Do you remember going to parties where you might have experimented with alcohol, cigarettes, drugs and/or sexual behaviours? Or having sexual feelings that you may have hidden and only explored in private? Or being secretly invited to a friend's house to look at 'dirty magazines'? And can you remember your first crush, your first relationship, the first time you held hands and kissed? Can you also remember the confusion and perhaps some angst?

Now, imagine how it is for adolescents growing up today, in the 21st century. The world is opening up to them. They are ready to explore and most are very excited to do so. They can easily communicate with people they like through fast, user-friendly online platforms, they can talk about what they like and don't like sexually, how they feel, what they want in a relationship and boundaries, without the embarrassment of a face-to-face conversation. They also have the opportunity to try out sexual scenarios online without any sexual health risks before they actually engage in any physical sexual behaviours with people offline. At the same time though, consider how it might feel to deal with your first sexual feelings when porn is available in just one click on a mobile phone. The confusion when hearing explicit song lyrics like Cardi B and Megan Thee Stallion's 'WAP' (WAP means Wet-Ass Pussy) and trying to work out if this is how you should behave when feeling sexual. This is the reality of growing up in the 21st century and a reality which is sometimes far away from the one we, as adults, experienced when growing up.

In the past 40 years the world has changed rapidly, and continues to do so, with technological innovations giving us many more opportunities to communicate and connect.

These changes have influenced our approach to and the content of relationships and sexuality education. As parents, carers and educators, we need to catch up with all these new digital possibilities in order to have a minimal level of understanding of our adolescents' lives. Even if we find porn, sexting and webcam sex unpalatable, we need to accept that these things are readily available and will be used by at least some of our teenagers as part of their sexual exploration and development. It's our task to give young people the support they need to develop the necessary skills to deal with these new opportunities in a way which suits them and that is safe.

Don't despair though, although digital technologies weren't part of our own adolescence, there are many aspects of adolescence that haven't changed. The confusion, excitement and uncertainty surrounding puberty, sexual feelings, romantic relationships, mood swings, the need for independence and so much more remains the same and we have all travelled that road. Despite the shift to a more digital world, the feelings remain the same. Some of the values and behaviours might have changed, but even these haven't changed completely, and they haven't changed for all.

Adolescence has always been a stage in which young people can be overwhelmed by a tsunami of feelings and thoughts. But today, a staggering number of expectations, demands, requests and 'must-dos' characterize young people's lives. As you may have recalled when we asked you to think back to your own adolescence, although this stage can be exciting, it can also be overwhelming at times.

Sometimes when we start a training session for parents, carers or teachers about relationships and sexuality education, we start by asking them to reflect on questions like: How did you feel as a teenager? What were the main questions you wanted answers to? What was your main worry? How close were you to your peers or to the adults who took care of you? How did you feel about your body? And about sexuality? Who were your closest friends and how do you perceive those friendships now? Did you masturbate? Can you remember your first sexual experience with someone else? Was this a positive or less positive experience? The reason we do this is to remind participants that it is too easy, when working or living with adolescents, to just see the challenges that (some) teenagers present. We can easily forget what being a teenager is like and some adults focus so much on correcting behaviours that the positive aspects of raising adolescents are pretty much forgotten. Young people can be incredibly strong, resilient, intelligent, creative, original and wise. They can also be insightful and, given the opportunity, they can discuss most points at an equal level as they mature. We can learn a great deal from adolescents. They are the future, they will be the change makers and they will manage our future planet. Isn't it wonderful that we can contribute to their development and their future lives?

This book

As you may know, this book is a follow-up to *Can I Have Babies Too?*, published in 2021, which was about relationships and sexuality education for children aged 0–11 years. When we had written that book, we were reminded by many of the readers that there was a need for a similar book that sensitively and comprehensively addressed the needs of young people in relation to relationships and sexuality education. So here it is, the follow-up for all of you who were impatiently waiting for answers and new information. For those of you who haven't read the first book please don't worry, this is a standalone book that can be read without having read *Can I Have Babies Too?*

The key message from our earlier book remains the same: relationships and sexuality education is best delivered as an integral part of everyday life, in informal everyday situations. However, our approach to adolescents is different. As children grow up, the number of external influences on their values, behaviours and knowledge grows. Teenagers look around, listen to others, draw their conclusions and develop their own values and opinions. If young people want information about sexuality, they can just look it up on the internet, they don't need to ask their parents or teachers everything anymore. Adults still need to inform, but their input needs to be led by the needs of the young person with a focus on enabling them to develop a set of competencies that can underpin positive sexual development and sexual well-being, namely:

- sexual literacy (having knowledge and confidence regarding the various aspects of sexuality)

- equitable attitudes regarding gender

- respect for human rights including an understanding of consent

- critical reflection skills

- coping and stress management

- interpersonal relationship skills.[1]

This book's prime focus is on supporting you to enable the young people in your lives to develop these competencies.

Who are we?

We are, first and foremost, parents of seven beautiful, awesome and sometimes terrible children. In addition to being parents we are also specialists in relationships and sexuality education.

Sanderijn van der Doef is a psychologist and sexologist, specializing in sexuality education for young children and adolescents. She has had a career in sexuality education for more than 30 years and is the author of several books for children, parents and teachers on sexuality education. Sanderijn worked for the Dutch Rutgers – the expertise centre for sexuality education in the Netherlands – for many years, including 15 years in the international department, developing programmes and giving training to local experts in Asia and Africa. Sanderijn is also a counsellor and works with children, parents and adults who experience sexual problems. Sexuality education is the motor that drives Sanderijn in her professional life, aiming to give all children and adolescents the opportunity to receive enough knowledge and skills about sexuality to feel confident to enjoy their sexual lives while being respectful to others.

Dr Clare Bennett is a senior lecturer at Cardiff University and a nurse with a background in sexual health. Her doctorate was about parent-child sexuality communication in the UK and she subsequently undertook further research on this topic in the Netherlands. Clare has published, taught and presented in this field internationally. She conducts research into various aspects of young people's sexual health promotion, the normalization of sexuality communication and the impact of sexually transmitted infections on quality of life. She also has an interest in young people's mental health. Clare's passion for comprehensive relationships and sexuality education comes from her clinical work as a nurse, caring for young people who did not have the necessary information and skills to make informed choices about relationships and their sexual behaviours.

Arris Lueks works at HAN University of Applied Sciences in the Netherlands, where she has taught thousands of trainee teachers how to introduce relationships and sexuality education into the primary school curriculum. Arris is experienced in teaching the Flag System (which we will discuss in Chapter 9), developed by Erika Frans from Sensoa, a Belgian expertise centre for sexual reproductive health. She also leads workshops on sexuality education for primary school teachers in the Netherlands and has given several workshops in the UK regarding relationships and sexuality education. Arris is committed to making sexuality a topic that everyone feels comfortable talking about.

Who is this book for?

We are aware that many books for parents and carers on how to give relationships and sexuality education to children already exist. Likewise, we are aware of the numerous training manuals and guides for professional educators on how to discuss sex and sexuality with their learners. Traditionally, informal (e.g. in the home) and formal (e.g. in schools) relationships and sexuality education have been seen as two separate entities, but we disagree with this separation. We believe that when it comes to learning about relationships and sexuality, young people don't see this divide, and when formal settings and informal settings work together young people benefit. So in this book we have brought the two contexts together. We want to improve the effectiveness of relationships and sexuality education for young people by focusing on the complementary role professionals and non-professionals have.

We have also found that adults in both formal and informal settings generally need the same kind of support: overcoming embarrassment, finding the right words and choosing the right approach. So, we have written this book for parents, grandparents, foster parents, carers, teachers, health care professionals, youth workers, social workers, young offender institute staff, counsellors, pedagogical workers and anyone else who cares for or works with young people. We consider anyone who discusses relationships and sexuality with children and adolescents as sexuality educators. Although we generally refer to readers collectively, on occasion we directly address parents and carers in this book, and at other times we directly address teachers. This doesn't mean other readers should feel ignored, it is just that on occasion, certain aspects of relationships and sexuality education are more likely to occur in the private space of the home or in school, and certain aspects require different handling depending upon the context.

We realize that families exist in many different compositions. Young people may grow up with a father and mother or with two parents of the same sex or with one parent. They may also grow up in extended families, in foster families or with stepparents. There are also young people who, for a variety of reasons, grow up in institutions. Regardless of the kind of home an adolescent grows up in, they have the right to support, safety and guidance. Taking care of children and adolescents means much more than providing a safe home, food and emotional care. It also means giving unconditional love, even in challenging situations. Every adolescent has the right to accurate, age and developmentally appropriate information to guide them in their search for answers to their questions. We hope that this book helps you to address these particular rights, regardless of the young person's family situation.

We also realize that our readers will have different backgrounds and different values. So have we. We are an international team of authors with international experience and we know that discussing relationships and sexuality with young people can be more or less challenging in different cultures. This book clearly has a European slant, with two of the three authors coming from the Netherlands where relationships and sexuality education is considered normal and useful. We have made some adaptations to suit the UK, US, Canadian and Australian context, but most of our Dutch and European ideas are still there.

Throughout the book, we share our individual values and opinions. Although we give you objective, evidence-based information, we cannot and do not want to be neutral. You may find our ideas about relationships and sexuality education different to your own and you may find what we say challenging or maybe even provocative. We do not intend to impose our values on you or to be prescriptive. Instead, we want to provide you with guidance and information based on research that shows what methods of relationships and sexuality education are effective and helpful for adolescents. How you apply this knowledge will be for you to decide, but we hope that you will approach the various chapters with an open mind.

With all of this in mind, this book is, of course, ultimately for young people, since we sincerely hope that everything you learn from it will enrich their lives. When we talk about adolescence we mean the World Health Organization (WHO)'s definition[2] which refers to the transitional phase of growth and development between childhood and adulthood, between the ages of 10 and 19. We also use the term 'adolescent' interchangeably with 'young person' and 'teenager' throughout the book.

So, what can you expect?

First of all, our book will be a positive book. Positive about adolescents and positive about relationships and sexuality education messages for this age group. Young people at this age are about to embark on a new stage in life, exploring romantic and sexual feelings and experimenting with relationships and sexual behaviours. They will benefit more if our messages are positive rather than focusing purely on warnings, prohibitions and risks. Growing up is a journey for young people in which they need to do a lot of 'self-learning'. We can support them in this by being less directive (i.e. telling them what to do) and more supportive in helping them make decisions that are right for them. Positivity, balanced with realism, will be the tone in this book.

Here's a short summary of the chapters that make up this book. In the first chapter we emphasize the importance of being in touch with your teenager. To really relate to them. We will explain that teenagers who feel that adults are genuinely interested in them and really connect with them are likely to have more confidence and be more willing to share questions and problems with that adult. In this first chapter we will also share an overview of some of the latest research findings about certain teen behaviours. We call this a 'reality check' and use this to tune you into the realities of life as a teenager today. Although the facts we present won't apply to all young people, they will give you an insight into the behaviours of many.

In the next chapter, Chapter 2, we discuss the concept of 'sexuality' and 'sexuality education' and the importance of these topics for adolescents. We explain why we prefer the term 'sexuality education' over 'sex education' and we discuss the goals we need to have in mind when engaging in relationships and sexuality education with teenagers. Of course, there are many goals that apply to relationships and sexuality education, for example to address any gaps in knowledge, to correct misinformation or to help young people build their own values and opinions around these topics. But for us, the main goal is to help young people in developing their critical thinking ability so that they can evaluate what it is right for them, whether solicited and unsolicited information they receive relating to relationships and sexuality is based on facts rather than 'fake-facts', whether consent is voluntary and so on. Critical thinking is extremely important for building autonomy and self-confidence and, in short, it is important for life.

Chapter 3 discusses different ways of communicating about relationships and sexuality with adolescents, both verbally and non-verbally, and we explain how some approaches are more effective than others. Chapter 4 is concerned with the brain development of teenagers and aims to help you better understand why young people behave and think as they do. By understanding this, hopefully you will be able to help and guide adolescents more effectively. The role of hormones and their influence on sexual feelings is discussed in Chapter 5, and the implications for adolescents' sexual behaviour and sexuality education are addressed.

Chapters 6, 7 and 8 are more practical. We have talked to many adults internationally about questions or topics they want help with discussing and we have used these as a basis for these chapters. We have divided the three chapters into three age groups, and we have related the specific questions to international guidelines and standards for sexuality education. In answering these questions we have drawn on our expertise as well as research data and the professional experience of sexuality educators around the world. But we have also tried to answer the questions or address the topics with a shared empathy, through our experience as parents and also as teachers of relationships and sexuality education. We know the ups and downs of parenting teenagers and we also know how different it is to give sexuality education to a class of students (relatively easy) compared to your own teenagers (sometimes less easy).

In Chapter 9 you will find an overview of an approach designed to assess whether to be concerned or otherwise about sexual situations that adolescents may be involved in and to respond appropriately, with the aim of promoting healthy sexual development. This approach is called the Flag System and we are grateful to Erika Frans of Sensoa for allowing us to include this excellent resource in our book.

Our hope is that you feel supported by this book and feel empowered to either start or to continue to communicate about relationships and sexuality with the young people in your lives. We also want you to be inspired by our passion for good quality relationships and sexuality education and to experience the benefits that emerge from having a trusting relationship with young people. But above all, we want you to learn how much fun relationships and sexuality education can be. As we said in our previous book: Don't limit your sexuality education to one talk and don't stop after one talk. Go beyond the talk and use everyday situations as a start or a reason to begin the conversation. See relationships and sexuality education as a process of continuous communication from infancy through to adulthood. Use everyday moments to connect with your teenager(s) and be aware that relationships and sexuality are inseparably interwoven with every part of a human being's life. From the day of birth to the end of life.

Enjoy the book and get in touch with us to share your stories on the JKP Blog (https://blog.jkp.com).

Sanderijn, Clare and Arris

Chapter 1

Being in touch

DOES 'GROWING UP' MEAN 'GROWING APART'?

Adolescence is a time of significant change with children rapidly morphing into young adults who are capable of making their own decisions and living largely independent lives. Bye bye little child, hello teenager! Although it is widely recognized that the accompanying changes that characterize adolescence can be bewildering for the young person, the same can be said for the adults who are involved in their lives. As they mature, young people often begin to use language that is unfamiliar to us as adults, they may change their appearance, they might want more independence and they are often influenced by their peers more than the adults in their lives. Your cute 12 year old can appear unrecognizable in just a matter of months, with parents, carers, teachers and other professionals struggling to keep up.

This chapter is all about being in touch with young people, which we acknowledge is no easy task. To help you begin to consider what 'being in touch' means, we invite you to reflect on the following scenarios:

Jane, who is 14 years old, decided to start dieting several months ago. After reading about her favourite singers' diets and following the vlogs of other girls her age who share their most successful diets, she selected one which she thought would be easy. She was allowed to eat everything she wanted to as long as she vomited everything up after eating. Her mother only started to notice that something was wrong once she had lost 10 kg (22 pounds). Her mother couldn't work out how she could be losing so much weight as she always participated in mealtimes and didn't appear to restrict her food intake. However, her mother didn't know what Jane was doing after eating.

Jonathan, who is 12 years old, had a secret online relationship with a man of 39. After 10 weeks of talking online, Jonathan decided to meet his friend in a cafe after school. Jonathan told his mother he would be home an hour later than usual as he wanted to finish his homework at school. His parents didn't know anything about his secret friendship.

These scenarios may have surprised you or they may resonate with you. You may have judged the parents negatively for being out of touch or you may have considered such scenarios an inevitable part of teenagers growing away from their parents. The first point to make is that these are true stories and the parents in each scenario cared deeply about their child. However, in both scenarios, the young person and their parents had lost touch with one another. This can happen very easily with children in secondary school making such huge adjustments and parents often being stretched in any number of ways.

Parents sometimes wonder how their children seem to change from being happy, cheerful kids to being shy, moody, under confident teenagers who only feel comfortable in baggy clothes and want to listen to depressing music. They sometimes perceive their teenagers' behaviour as hostile and back off because they get fed up of being hurt and rejected. However, these changes often simply reflect the pressure that many young people feel under to adapt to their changing circumstances and others' expectations constantly. Some teenagers tell us that coming home from school can feel like returning from the battlefield and all they want is a safe place at home where they are accepted and loved. Knowing that their parent or carer knows who they are, what they feel, what they like and dislike and still loves them and appreciates them gives young people the ultimate feeling of safety. This isn't always easy though.

Growing up doesn't necessarily mean that adolescents grow apart from the adults in their lives, but staying connected requires significant energy and commitment from carers and parents. At this stage, it's not unusual for young people to prefer their peers' company to their parents'/carers' and many are glued to their phones and computers and may want to spend hours in their bedroom. However, research shows that the well-being of young people is positively influenced by being connected to parents and carers.[1] The next section of this chapter aims to help you assess how well connected you are with your adolescent or those who you work with.

A quick test

Here's a quick test to check how much you know about your teenager's life or the lives of the young people you work with. Try to answer all the questions that are relevant to your situation. Keep your notes safe as we will ask you to repeat the test after completing this book and you'll need to compare your two sets of answers. Throughout the questions we have referred to a teenager as 'they' or 'your child/teenager'. But you may be thinking about just one teenager, perhaps your son or granddaughter, or you may be thinking about a whole class full of young people or perhaps a caseload – just personalize the questions to you and your context:

1. Do you know the name of your teenager's best friend?

   a. Yes, it's ...
   b. I know my child has friends, but I don't know their names
   c. I don't know

2. Has your teenager ever experienced bullying (either being bullied or bullying others)?

   a. I know for sure they have/haven't
   b. I think they have/haven't, but I'm not sure
   c. I don't know

3. Has your teenager ever drunk alcohol?

   a. I know for sure they have/haven't
   b. I think they have/haven't, but I'm not certain
   c. I don't know

4. Has your teenager ever smoked cigarettes?

   a. I know for sure they have/haven't
   b. I think they have/haven't, but I'm not certain
   c. I don't know

5. Has your teenager ever tried drugs?

   a. I know for sure they have/haven't
   b. I think they have/haven't, but I'm not certain
   c. I don't know

6. Is your child usually happy?

   a. I'm sure they are/aren't
   b. I think they are/aren't, but I'm not sure
   c. I don't know

7. Has your child ever been in love?

   a. I know for sure they have/haven't
   b. I think they have/haven't, but I'm not sure
   c. I don't know

8. Does your child masturbate?

   a. I know for sure they do/don't
   b. I think they do/don't, but I'm not sure
   c. I don't know

9. Do you know whether your teenager has ever watched porn?

   a. I know for sure they have/haven't
   b. I think they have/haven't, but I'm not sure
   c. I don't know

10. Has your child ever engaged in sexual behaviour with someone else?

    a. I know for sure they have/haven't
    b. I think they have/haven't, but I'm not sure
    c. I don't know

11. Has your child ever had negative experiences with sexuality?

    a. I know for sure they have/haven't
    b. I think they have/haven't, but I'm not sure
    c. I don't know

Were you able to answer all the questions or were some of your answers 'I don't know'? The more confident you were in giving your answers (even if these answers weren't positive) the more you know about your child. Knowing about your adolescent's daily life experiences is important to make them feel seen and acknowledged. Later in this chapter under the heading 'Reality check' we will discuss what research has identified regarding these behaviours among teenagers – you may find this helpful in broadening your understanding of teenagers' lives.

Of course though, knowing a lot about the lives of teenagers isn't enough to make them feel acknowledged. The way adults react to what they know about young people also has an impact on how safe they feel with the adults in their lives and their well-being. We'll return to this theme later in the book.

The importance of a warm family climate

In our previous book *Can I Have Babies Too?*, we introduced the term 'warm family climate'. Researchers[2] define a warm family climate or warm family environment as having three aspects: being supportive, monitoring and using the right level of control. We consider a warm family climate as an environment in which children are surrounded by people who are supportive and interested in them, who are aware of what is going on with them and who can set the right limits and boundaries to a child's behaviour. If a child has adults around them who show an interest in their life and their emotions, they are more likely to be willing to share their worries, questions and experiences with them. Research also shows that adolescents who grow up in a warm family climate with positive adolescent-parent relationships are happier,[3] have greater self-confidence[4] and experience healthier sexual development.[5] With regards to 'healthy sexual development' we are referring to adolescents who are at ease with their sexuality and emerging sexual feelings and who feel empowered with the knowledge to take healthy and responsible decisions concerning their sexuality with respect to others.

In creating a 'warm family climate' the constitution of the family doesn't matter; the number of adults and their individual sexual orientations and gender are irrelevant as long as there is unconditional love and positive attention for the young person. A single parent family can give as much love as a family with two, three or four parents. A stepparent, grandparent, non-biological parent or any other adult who plays a consistent role in the young person's life can make a young person feel loved, appreciated and safe. However, feeling safe is only possible when certain conditions are met, namely:

- A young person shouldn't be exposed to any physical or mental threat or harm.

- A young person's worries are heard and never ignored by the adults who are special to them.

- A young person is accepted for what they are, even if their behaviour is not necessarily accepted, which is what we mean by 'unconditional love'.

Showing interest, respecting privacy and building autonomy

A warm family climate doesn't mean that adults have to know everything about their teenager's life. When children grow up, their need for privacy also grows. Some teenagers don't want to share everything with their parents, others do until they start their first intimate relationship, and others might want to continue to share most things throughout all of their teenage years. It entirely depends upon the individual teenager but most do want some degree of privacy. For instance, they may start to close their bedroom door and if they share their bedroom they may ask for or make a room-divider. Some will start to keep a private diary, others may want privacy when chatting or connecting with friends and others may look for privacy outside the home and want to go out every evening to meet friends.

Many carers and parents find this transition quite difficult, especially if they previously enjoyed a confiding relationship with their child. Sometimes they feel that their child no longer likes them and is rejecting them. But a desire for privacy among teenagers is an important step in their development because it's associated with the need to become more independent and, particularly, with the development of autonomy. Autonomy refers to the adolescent's increasing ability to think, feel, act and make decisions on their own. This process of autonomy building is a key aspect of adolescence. When this process fails or is hampered, there is a risk that the young person may struggle to function in aspects of adulthood, especially in relation to intimate relationships.[6]

Autonomy and independence are slightly different things. Independence generally refers to a teen's capacity to behave on their own and is part of becoming autonomous. Autonomy means thinking, feeling and making decisions that are truly one's own rather than going along with what others believe. Autonomy is important in the development of decision-making skills, self-reliance and the ability to resist peer pressure. Healthy adults are autonomous functioning people who show confidence in their thoughts and behaviours.[7]

Supporting teenagers in becoming independent and in developing their autonomy means giving them the privacy they need, yet at the same time, showing an interest in their daily life. This can be quite a challenge! It means giving privacy, but not abandoning them. It means motivating them to find solutions for their problems themselves but also offering your support. It also means accepting their decisions even when you don't agree with them and finding a balance between giving them enough space and, at the same time, setting clear boundaries. An example of this might be: *'OK, you can meet up with your friend, but I want you back at 10pm sharp.'* While none of this is easy, the investment is worthwhile as your actions will demonstrate both respect and trust for your child.

What kind of 'parenting style' does an adolescent need?

In our previous book, we explained the importance of reflecting on 'parenting styles' which refer to the different ways parents, carers and other educators interact with children and young people. Different parenting styles have been researched in relation to their effect on the well-being of children and young people. One particular parenting style, the 'Emotion Coach Parent', which comes from the work of John Gottman,[8] can be particularly helpful in supporting young people to become increasingly autonomous. An Emotion Coach is aware of and values the young person's emotions and uses these as an opportunity to become close to them. This kind of adult doesn't make fun of the young person's feelings and doesn't tell them how they should feel. Instead, emotional moments are considered as opportunities to listen to the young person and for the adult to help them label and manage their feelings. The Emotion Coach helps the young person to solve the problem which has led to their heightened emotions. This kind of adult helps young people to trust their feelings and find solutions for their problems. In this way, young people have the opportunity to develop high self-esteem and have healthier interactions with others.[9]

Let's have a look at how an Emotion Coach might deal with some typical adolescent behaviour:

Robert, age 15, comes home from school. He throws his shoes and jacket on the floor and runs upstairs without greeting his dad.

Father: *'Hello! What's the rush?'*

Robert: *'Nothing. Need to do my homework.'* Robert slams his bedroom door.

The father's first emotion is anger as there is a clear rule in their household that when the children come home from school, they say hello and put their shoes and coats in the cupboard where they belong. But once he calms down he can see that something is wrong with Robert. He is mad, frustrated or upset about something. He decides to leave him alone for a while as he understands the slam of the bedroom door to mean 'leave me alone'. After 15 minutes he makes Robert a drink, goes upstairs and knocks on his door. He hears Robert murmur something and he goes into his bedroom. He is lying on his bed playing a game on his phone.

Father: *'I've got a drink for us. Let's sit and talk.'*

Robert is silent and doesn't move.

Father: *'It looks like something's happened today. Do you want to talk about it?'*

Again Robert just murmurs something but doesn't move.

Father: *'Here, have your drink before it goes cold. Have you had an argument? Was someone unkind? Did you do badly in your test? What's happened?'*

Robert explains that on his way home he saw a girl who he has a crush on talking to his best friend George. They were looking into each other's eyes, smiling at each other and flirting. This is exactly what he had wanted to do with this girl but hadn't had the nerve to. Now, it was too late because George had got her attention even though he knew Robert fancied her.

Father: *'Oh, that must feel awful. It feels bad, right?'*

Robert nods and his dad sees tears in his eyes. After sitting silently next to Robert with his arms around him, his dad says: *'How can I help you feel better?'*

Robert doesn't know, he just needs to be sad for a while and appreciates his father's presence: *'Don't go dad, just stay with me for a while. Until I feel a bit better.'*

The Emotion Coach parenting style has similar principles to those seen in positive psychology parenting. In positive psychology the view on parenting is that it requires a warm, positive, caring, empowering interaction with the child or young person, without being permissive or authoritarian. It is concerned with setting boundaries and supporting the young person's behaviour through open communication with a focus on their needs and emotions. Positive parenting styles[10] encourage a young person's autonomy by:

- supporting exploration and involvement in decision making

- paying attention and responding to the young person's needs

- using effective communication

- attending to the young person's emotional expression and control

- rewarding and encouraging positive behaviours

- providing clear rules and expectations

- applying consistent consequences for behaviours

- providing adequate supervision and monitoring

- acting as a positive role model

- making positive family experiences a priority.

Positive parents support a young person's growth by being loving, supportive, firm, consistent and involved. Such parents go beyond communicating their expectations by being positive role models for their children to emulate.

There are other parenting styles which include similar principles to positive parenting, one of which is the 'authoritative parenting style'.[11] This is an approach that includes a good balance of the following parenting qualities:

- assertive, but not intrusive

- demanding, but responsive

- supportive in terms of discipline, but not punitive.[12]

A Dutch study shows that this kind of parenting style is particularly supportive for the healthy sexual development of children and adolescents.[13] These findings have also been supported in other international studies.[14] Being clear, warm and supportive but, at the same time, setting limits in combination with an open attitude towards the sexual development of young people and open communication seems to support adolescents in being more satisfied with their own sexuality and experiencing fewer sexual problems than children raised with other parenting approaches.[15] In addition, role modelling significantly influences adolescents' relational behaviours.[16]

Parental monitoring means being interested in and giving genuine attention and guidance to a child or young person. It has been shown that parental monitoring can have a positive impact on young people's alcohol, drugs and cigarette use, resistance to peer pressure and on adolescent sexual well-being.[17]

In summary, positive parenting can enhance young people's health and sexual development when it includes:

- awareness of the young person's emotions

- warm interaction

- interest in the young person's needs

- monitoring the young person's daily preferences and behaviours without being controlling

- open communication about relationships and sexuality

- an open attitude towards the adolescent's sexual development

- positive role modelling from parents and carers.

Reality check

Earlier in this chapter we invited you to complete some questions to help you check how much you know about your adolescent(s). We now want to share the findings of some research with you regarding young people's behaviours. You might find some of the data shocking and some may be reassuring. If you are a parent or carer, reflect on the data and compare the findings with your own adolescent's daily life. You could also use the research findings as a starting point for a discussion with your child. You could ask them about their thoughts on these topics and whether the findings are in keeping with their friends' and perhaps their own experiences. Regardless of the answers, don't judge, just show your interest in your teenager's observations and perceptions.

Happiness

Several reports[18] have identified that young people from Finland, Switzerland and the Netherlands are among the happiest in the world, with young people from the UK, Australia, Canada and the US feeling less satisfied with their lives. Factors contributing to young people's happiness were identified as having friends, an absence of bullying, a supportive home and school environment and academic expectations that weren't too high. In addition, Ruut Veenhoven, the 'Happiness Professor', suggests that happiness may be attributed to parenting styles with the Dutch and Danes placing a priority on becoming independent rather than on sticking to the rules.[19]

The WHO/HBSC (Health Behaviour in School-aged Children) study,[20] which was conducted in 45 countries in Europe and North America, shows that mental well-being declines with age during adolescence, with girls reporting poorer mental well-being than boys. Nervousness, irritability and sleep difficulties are the most common complaints mentioned among the 227,441 young people aged 11, 13 and 15 years who took part in this study. Younger adolescents are also more likely to become victims of bullying at school, especially cyberbullying among girls, with bullying declining as adolescents grow older.

Alcohol use

The WHO/HBSC study[21] identified that around 23% of 11 year olds and 47% of 13 year olds in the UK had previously consumed alcohol, which can be a predictor of alcohol abuse later in life.[22] One in five 15 year olds (20%) had been drunk twice or more in their lifetime, and almost one in seven (15%) had been drunk in the last 30 days. Drunkenness was more common among boys than girls in all age groups in around a third of countries/regions in the study at ages 11 and 15, with the only exception being Wales (UK) where girls had a higher prevalence of drunkenness both throughout their lifetime and in the last 30 days.[23] In the United States,[24] although young people drink less often than adults do, when they do drink, they drink more and over 90% of all alcoholic drinks consumed by young people are consumed through binge drinking.

Cigarette smoking

In the WHO/HBSC study[25] outlined above, across all ages 15% of boys and 13% of girls reported having smoked cigarettes and 7% of boys and girls reported having smoked in the last 30 days. However, cigarette smoking has decreased among 11–15 year olds in the past ten years.[26] In the USA,[27] approximately 20% of high school students reported having smoked cigarette products.

Drug use

In Europe almost one in seven adolescents (13%) aged 15 reported having used cannabis, with a higher prevalence among boys (15%) than girls (11%).[28] Use of cannabis in the last 30 days was reported by 7% of 15 year olds.[29] In the USA, approximately 15% of young people between 12 and 17 years reported having used cannabis and 7% of that age group had used it in the past month.[30] An Australian study reported that 22% of 14–19 year olds had used an illicit drug and 16% of the boys and 15% of the girls had done so recently.[31]

Watching porn

A survey in the UK[32] identified that 48% of the 11–16 year old participants had seen online pornography, with the older age groups more likely to have seen it. In a study in the USA,[33] 8% of 12–17 year olds were watching porn daily, 18% weekly and 11% once or twice a month. In a further study conducted in Australia just under half of all the children who participated, aged 9–16 years, reported having seen pornographic images, either intentionally or unintentionally.[34]

Being in love

In question 7, we asked whether your child had ever been in love. What did you assume we meant by this? Did you think we meant a special relationship without sexual behaviour or something else? We were deliberately unclear in the hope that we might prompt you to consider these kinds of questions.

In a Dutch study,[35] most (79%) young people reported having experienced feelings of romantic love by the age of 12, with approximately 3% reporting having experienced these feelings for someone of the same sex or both sexes. Another Dutch study[36] identified that children between 12 and 15 years are more concerned with romantic feelings and non-sexual behaviours, like holding hands, kissing on the lips or cheeks or sitting close to each other. These patterns of behaviour continue up to around age 15–16 when sexual feelings tend to increase. A study in the USA[37] found that by the age of 17 approximately 70% of participants had had some experience of a romantic relationship. In Australia, a study[38] identified that by 16–17 years of age, two-thirds of the young people surveyed had had experience with romantic relationships and 4% had had a date with someone of the same sex.

Masturbation

From a Dutch national survey[39] we know that by the age of 15-17, 85% of the boys and 38% of the girls who participated had experienced masturbation. According to the Australian 2018 National Survey of Secondary Students and Sexual Health,[40] by the age of 16-17 around 96% of boys had had experience of masturbation with fewer girls (83%) reporting the same. We don't know how common masturbation is in other countries due to a lack of published research but we do know that this difference across the genders continues through to adulthood. As we discuss in the next chapters we appreciate that many adults find masturbation particularly embarrassing and difficult to discuss. However, masturbation can help young people in learning about their own bodies and what they like and don't like. In turn, this can help young people in developing their confidence in relation to sexual relationships as they mature.[41]

Sexual relationships

In the WHO/HBSC study,[42] it was identified that by age 15 around one in four boys and one in seven girls reported having had sexual intercourse, with less than 60% reporting having used one of the two most reliable contraceptive methods – the pill or condom (or both). According to the Pew Research Center,[43] in the USA approximately 36% of 15-17 year olds reported having had a sexual relationship. In the UK, the British National Survey of Sexual Attitudes[44] identified a median age of 16 for first sexual intercourse.

Negative experiences with sexuality

Negative experiences with sexuality can be a range of different experiences varying from sexual bullying, sexual harassment and sexual abuse, to having experienced a sexually transmitted infection or an unplanned pregnancy. All of these things can happen to adolescents anywhere in the world, sometimes without parents, carers and teachers knowing. Some children and adolescents feel they can't or don't want to share such experiences and suffer alone. Some may not show any obvious signs of distress but others might behave in a way that is out of character for them. Every teenager's response to negative sexual experiences differs and it is hard to provide a list of common signals. Regular checking or monitoring of their well-being is appropriate and helpful, but if you feel that there is something troubling your child or a young person that you teach and they do not wish to share, please consult a professional.

Summary

In this chapter we have given you an insight into the reality of adolescents' lives today. Everything we've written about won't necessarily apply to your child or to every young person in your class, but aspects might and they certainly will apply to other young people. As parents, carers and teachers it's helpful to keep these facts in mind when supporting adolescents throughout their journey towards adulthood.

Some key messages we gave include:

- To enable adolescents to develop into independent autonomous young adults, giving and showing unconditional love is important. Whatever they do, whatever they say, they need to know that you will continue to love them. Not because of how they behave or what they achieve, but because of who they are.

- Monitoring and checking their well-being as well as talking about their everyday lives with them enables young people to know that they are seen and acknowledged.

- Although the realities of young people that we presented in this chapter may not apply directly to the teenagers in your lives, their friends and peers may have had these experiences which may indirectly affect your child or the young people in your class.

- Beliefs, attitudes and values concerning parenting or educating styles impact directly upon the development of young people.

In the next chapters we'll discuss some of the challenges and opportunities you may face in discussing sexuality with adolescents.

Chapter 2

Challenges and opportunities in discussing sexuality with adolescents

Over the years young people have asked us numerous questions about sexuality, for example whether the size and shape of their breasts or penises are normal, why they feel the way they do, whether they may be pregnant and what to do, whether they might have an infection, how to deal with abuse, how to break up and remain friends, among many other important questions. You can probably relate to this list and add a few other questions yourself.

All questions are important to young people and they deserve accurate, factual responses. Sometimes it can be challenging to find the right words but these conversations provide a fantastic opportunity for a meaningful conversation. By this stage the majority of young people will have received some kind of relationships and sexuality education at school, but for many there may still be gaps in their knowledge and understanding. So, checking their needs and wants is important. Take this (real) example of three adolescent girls who all thought they may be pregnant: one had had oral sex with her boyfriend, one had had unprotected vaginal sex one day after her period had finished and the third had had unprotected vaginal sex and had forgotten to take her contraceptive pill that evening. These girls were intelligent and bright and all three had received the basics of sexuality education at school. But they lacked specific knowledge about their bodies and reproduction. Similarly, we've had questions from very smart boys that clearly demonstrate a lack of understanding about fundamental aspects of sexuality.

For these young people and many others like them, their sexuality education was insufficient because it hadn't given them the information they required. In this chapter we explore why relationships and sexuality education based on the needs of the young person is so necessary, why it should be comprehensive and what we mean by this.

Challenge 1: Do we have the same aim in mind? Sex or sexuality?

One particular challenge in sexuality education is language. Have you noticed that we use the term 'sexuality education' rather than 'sex education'? The latter is frequently used in schools, books, movies and even by some experts, but we have very deliberately decided to make a clear distinction between the two terms in this book. For us 'sex' refers to behaviours and acts which (should) give a pleasurable, positive feeling. 'Sexuality', however, is much more than this. No agreed definition of sexuality exists internationally, although the World Health Organization offers the following 'working definition':

> a central aspect of being human throughout life encompasses sex, gender identities and roles, sexual orientation, eroticism, pleasure, intimacy and reproduction. Sexuality is experienced and expressed in thoughts, fantasies, desires, beliefs, attitudes, values, behaviours, practices, roles and relationships. While sexuality can include all of these dimensions, not all of them are always experienced or expressed. Sexuality is influenced by the

interaction of biological, psychological, social, economic, political, cultural, legal, historical, religious and spiritual factors.[1]

Sexuality, therefore, encompasses:

- Physical aspects: Our bodies, how we look and express ourselves, age-related changes to our bodies.

- Emotional aspects: Love, attraction, happiness, pleasure, jealousy, disappointment, sadness, nervousness, sexual arousal.

- Relational aspects: Bonds between two (or more) people, marriage, friendship.

- Behavioural aspects: Kissing, hugging, touching, holding hands, writing messages, sexual intercourse or other sexual behaviours (alone or with others), sexual harassment, abuse.

- Consequences of behaviours: Happiness, pregnancy, emotional bonding, infection, abortion, reproduction.

- Gender aspects: Gender (in)equality, gender stereotypes, how people feel about being a girl or a boy or another gender, gender identity whether transgender or cisgender (cisgender is a person whose gender identity matches their sex assigned at birth), gender fluidity, sexual identity, sexual orientation, LGBTIQ+ (lesbian, gay, bisexual, transgender, intersex and queer/ questioning).

- Cultural aspects: Ideas about sexuality that have a cultural origin and can vary between and within different cultures.

- Religious aspects: Expectations, norms or 'rules' about masturbation, abortion, sex before marriage or the purpose of intercourse.

- Legal aspects: 'Age of consent', laws on consent and abuse/rape, laws about sexual relationships between adults and children.

- Values: Personal values, cultural values and/or religious values about what is right or wrong, appropriate or inappropriate.

Because 'sex' and 'sexuality' are used interchangeably, and to clarify the difference between the two, we suggest you develop a 'Sexuality Mind Map' which you may find useful to do yourself, with your partner, with friends or with young people. You simply develop a mind map with the term 'sexuality' in the centre and write down everything that comes to mind when you think of the concept. What comes out is a personal (or group) interpretation of what sexuality means. There are no right or wrong answers and everyone will have their own interpretation, based on their personal background and individual context. In our experience, although people's mind maps might look different, they make the same point – sexuality encompasses much more than just sexual intercourse.

This is why we prefer the term 'sexuality education'. In the same way that sex is just one aspect of sexuality, sex education is only one aspect of sexuality education.

Challenge 2: Do we want to achieve the same thing?

'Comprehensive sexuality education' or 'CSE' focuses on much more than sex.

CSE covers a broad range of issues relating to both the physical and biological aspects of sexuality and the emotional and social aspects. It recognizes and accepts all people as sexual beings and is concerned with more than just the prevention of disease or pregnancy. CSE programmes should be adapted to the age and stage of development of the target group.[2]

Although controversies exist internationally about the term 'comprehensive' and CSE as a term is mostly used in formal settings like schools, this is our preferred term for the purposes of this book. So, what does CSE aim to achieve? Why, as experts, are we trying to motivate parents, carers, teachers and other professionals to communicate about sexuality with children and adolescents and what do we want the impact of CSE to be on young people?

Research from all over the world[3] has demonstrated that good-quality CSE is effective in giving children and young people the necessary information and tools to make responsible and healthy decisions regarding their own sexuality. Examples might include: knowing when they are ready for sexual relationships; knowing what to do when a sexual relationship or a sexual behaviour doesn't feel right for them; being open minded with regard to sexual diversity; being respectful of others' preferences when they differ to their own; and knowing how to protect themselves and their partner against unplanned pregnancies and sexually transmitted infections.

For young people to make responsible, healthy decisions, they need to have reliable information about the various aspects of sexuality. This is quite different to 'information' that is based on opinion or popular beliefs. Young people also need to develop their own attitudes and values which, again, need to be underpinned by accurate information. Values will never be fixed; they may change over time or in response to specific situations. Young people listen, observe and read what others have to say and this shapes their values, temporarily or for a longer period. Parents and carers have a significant influence on the development of children's values in the first 12 years of the child's life, but peers and role models become increasingly important during adolescence, meaning that young people may develop values that are in opposition to their family's. Although this can be difficult for parents and carers, it's important to remember that differing values can be a good basis for discussion and mutual learning. Additionally, being clear and explicit about your values and explaining why you think this way will increase the chance of young people adopting similar values since they are better able to understand why the specific value is important.

Knowledge and values alone are not enough though; young people also need to learn skills. For example, how to say and respect 'no' or 'yes', to engage and interact in a kind and respectful way with others and to become resilient in the context of negative and threatening situations. To develop these kinds of skills, young people need the space to try out different behaviours and to experiment. They also need the opportunity to make mistakes, because this is how they learn how to do things better next time.

In other words, young people need to develop certain competencies[4] to become sexually healthy and to reach sexual well-being. Examples of these competencies are:

- sexual literacy (having knowledge and confidence regarding the various aspects of sexuality)

- equitable attitudes regarding gender

- respect for human rights including an understanding of consent

- critical reflection skills

- coping and stress management

- interpersonal relationship skills.

For us, this is what sexuality education should be about: supporting young people in developing these competencies. Relationships and sexuality education (or CSE) should support young people in understanding relevant facts, it should help them develop their attitudes and values and it should enable them to develop skills. To achieve these aims, it takes more than one standalone lesson at school, a single chapter in a book or an isolated talk by a parent or carer. It takes years of conversations, debates, role modelling and support, as well as courage on the part of adults to let young people gradually start to make their own decisions, to enjoy successes and, equally, to make mistakes as this is what is required for young people to know 'this is who I am and this is what I want'. This is what we have tried to help you achieve in writing this book.

Challenge 3: Your values

Values are an important aspect of relationships and sexuality and, therefore, relationships and sexuality education. However, the way we convey our values can pose a challenge if we're not self-aware. Young children learn values from adults who are close to them and, as they grow older, from other adults such as teachers. However, as they progress to become teenagers, peers' values and opinions become more relevant.[5] This doesn't mean that your influence as a parent, carer or teacher is redundant though. Even if it sometimes feels like that, many of your messages, intended or otherwise, stay with them – sometimes more than you think!

For this reason, it's important to reflect on your personal values and to take a moment to reflect on the kinds of values you wish to convey to the young people around you, why you wish to convey them, whether these values align with your behaviours and whether your verbal messages are supported by your actions. We rarely get the opportunity to reflect on how we feel about sexuality and the topics that it encompasses, but to become effective relationships and sexuality educators, an understanding of our own values and associated behaviours is key because we will inevitably convey them to young people.

Although we refer to parents, carers and educators synonymously throughout the chapter, when considering values, the two roles deviate slightly. The educator's role is to help children to understand an issue and to develop their own personal ideas about the topic, whereas parents might also wish to convey their personal or family values to their child. Parents absolutely have the right to do this and it's part of their role, even if their values are different to those promoted in the child's school or in this book. Values are personal, and although people will inevitably have different perspectives and disagree with each other, everyone has the right to have their own values and opinions. For professional educators though, our advice would be to focus on factual information as much as possible and to encourage children to develop their own values and opinions as much as possible, based on the factual information they receive from you. This doesn't mean that you have to be totally neutral, but it's about giving young people the opportunity to build their own values based on a range of factual information that they receive from you. In Chapter 7 (topics 3 and 5) we give some examples of exercises which teachers can use to explain how to build values based on correct factual information.

Here's an activity for you to do to encourage you to think through your opinions regarding different values that adults have shared with us in our work. It can be done as a parent or teacher or you can do the activity with your partner or with friends. It could be the start of a discussion or just a personal reflection. First, decide on whether you agree or disagree with the statements in the following table and complete the first column to indicate your response. Next, decide on which statements are important for you to convey to young people. The statements are from different sources and may not be true or factual.

	Agree [✓] or disagree [✗]?	Important to convey to young people? Yes [✓] or No [✗]?
Sex and love belong together	☐	☐
Everyone has the right to experience sexuality in their own way as long as it's not harmful to others	☐	☐
There are more genders than just male and female	☐	☐
All genders are equal	☐	☐
Gender is fluid (meaning people's gender identities may change during their lifetime)	☐	☐
It's OK for my child to be transgender	☐	☐
Boys and girls are different from birth and should be treated differently	☐	☐
Girls should be careful if they choose to look 'sexy'	☐	☐
Sexual behaviour with a partner should be delayed until marriage	☐	☐
Sexual behaviour is fine when there is no love	☐	☐
Men and women have different sexual desires and needs	☐	☐
People should respect others' boundaries	☐	☐
Young people shouldn't feel embarrassed for having sexual feelings	☐	☐
Young people shouldn't feel embarrassed for not having sexual feelings	☐	☐

cont.

	Agree [✓] or disagree [✗]?	Important to convey to young people? Yes [✓] or No [✗]?
Parents should agree with each other about the content of sexuality education for their child	☐	☐
Fathers should be involved in sexuality education for both their sons and daughters	☐	☐
Sexual diversity is a normal part of sexuality education	☐	☐
Homosexuality is OK	☐	☐
Homosexuality is OK for my own child	☐	☐
Sexuality education for teenagers is best given at school	☐	☐
Sexuality education should be introduced to children from a young age	☐	☐
Sexuality education should be taught to girls and boys separately	☐	☐
Porn is inappropriate for adolescents	☐	☐
Faithfulness in a relationship is essential	☐	☐
Oral sex isn't real sex	☐	☐
Anal sex is dirty and abnormal	☐	☐
Add in any other statements that you think are important to consider:	☐	☐
_____	☐	☐
_____	☐	☐

How did you find this? Did you find that you were absolutely clear about your position on some statements and less so on others? When you look back to when you were younger, do you think your values and opinions have changed? Are you able to identify why you hold these values, why you agree/disagree, why you think certain statements are true or untrue and correct or incorrect? These kind of 'why questions' will help you identify the reasons behind your feelings and values, and by making them explicit this will help you to explain why you hold particular values. Or sometimes, this process can help you identify that your values are based on moral or cultural arguments that you grew up with and messages conveyed in popular media, and that you may wish to question them.

Giving yourself space to reflect on your values is important because they will impact upon what you say to young people and they will also influence your behaviours. A simple example is menstruation. Have you ever noticed yourself using different words when explaining menstruation to a teenager, depending upon their sex and age? Have you found yourself using language that conveys your own personal experiences of menstruation or observed experiences of your sister or mother, for example 'painful', 'anxiety', 'embarrassing', 'exciting', 'healthy', 'normal' etc.? Even if you try to stay neutral have you noticed how young people have picked up on non-verbal messages conveyed through your eyes or body language? Previous experiences often shape how we explain or talk about sensitive, intimate or very personal topics.

Another suggestion that can be very helpful in checking out where your values and opinions have come from is to reflect on your own sexual history. We appreciate that this can be challenging for some people and we don't want you to feel pressured to do this, but it is helpful to do so if you are able, because your past is the foundation of your current life. Even if people try to forget past experiences (both good and bad), memories can still occasionally come to mind and influence what is expressed, both verbally and non-verbally.

So, if you feel that this is a safe thing for you to do, draw a horizontal timeline from birth to the present and divide it into five year sections. Next, in the corresponding sections write down any memories that you have regarding relationships and sexuality. These can be both positive and negative. Examples could be your first memory of being called a boy, a girl or your first memory of not feeling like either – how did you feel – positive, negative or neutral? Likewise, playing 'doctors' with a friend, being touched intimately, falling in love for the first time, your first romantic relationship, your memories of experiencing masturbation and orgasm, experiences of sexual intercourse, and so on. How did these experiences make you feel – positive, negative or neutral? Once you have listed all of these experiences, take some time to reflect on the impact of these experiences on your ideas about sexuality, other people, your body, your expectations about relationships and your opinions regarding sexual behaviours.

Taking some time to think about where your ideas have come from might help you figure out why you think about sexuality as you currently do. Regardless of whether these thoughts have made you sad, happy or a mixture of both, your past history is likely to have had an impact upon your motives, values and behaviours regarding relationships and sexuality education.[6] This kind of self-awareness can help you become a more effective sexuality educator because being aware of where your fears or confidence may come from can help you evaluate whether your messages are truly beneficial in meeting the needs of young people.

A suggestion to use with a partner, friends, colleagues or young people is to make a list of messages about sexuality, gender and relationships that they remember receiving in the past from their parents, teachers, peers and other influences. You may find this useful too. If so, take some time now to consider what messages you received regarding these issues as you were growing up. Which of these messages would you like to keep and pass on to young people and which do you think are best forgotten? What new messages would you also like to give to teenagers?

Being aware of your opinions and values related to relationships and sexuality will enable you to distinguish between facts and what you personally believe. This doesn't mean that you must always be neutral when giving sexuality education, but being aware of how your values will permeate every verbal and non-verbal message you give about relationships and sexuality can help you in deciding when you want to be explicit about your own opinions and when to stick to factual information.

Challenge 4: Discussing sexuality at home

When children are young, parents who are reluctant to discuss sexuality with their children use arguments like *'my child is too young for this'*, but once children go to secondary school, we often hear parents saying *'school can do a better job than me'* or *'they don't need to hear it from me, they know it all anyway'*. For some young people, the input they receive from school on relationships and sexuality education is the only input that they receive beyond what they learn from peers, the internet and observing the world around them. But we know that the quality of relationships and sexuality education varies considerably from school to school, and even when it is excellent, young people's learning about sexuality doesn't stop when the final bell rings at the end of the school day.

Openly communicating about relationships and sexuality at home has several opportunities and benefits. It enables young people to feel safe to ask questions, to discuss these topics and to develop their knowledge and understanding. It also allows you to increase the bond between you and your teenager because having these conversations shows them that you are interested in their lives, especially if you do this in a non-judgemental way.

It is worth emphasizing here that talking with your teenagers about sexuality will not encourage them to have sex. In fact, research shows that talking about relationships and sexuality with children and young people often results in delayed sexual debut.[7]

Even if parents or carers choose not to discuss sexuality with their teenagers, they will still convey messages and inadvertently educate their children. For example, silence may be interpreted as 'we disapprove', 'we don't want to hear about this aspect of your life' or perhaps 'sexuality is something to feel awkward about'. Equally, parents' and carers' behaviours will have been observed and internalized by young people. For example, the way in which they interact with other adults and their partners, the jokes they make about relationships and sexuality, their reactions to television programmes that include diverse relationships and sexualities will have all been interpreted as messages.

If left alone without any support or communication, young people can unwittingly access information that is, at best, misleading. Feelings of isolation are common at this stage, and if young people don't have the opportunity to express their concerns or to discuss their feelings, their sense of isolation will only be exacerbated. Teenagers can easily feel confused and anxious about the physical and mental changes that they experience as they mature as well as their sexual feelings. We have seen this too many times in our work, with young people getting to a point of crisis because they think that they are the only person to have ever felt attracted to someone of the same sex, to have asymmetrical genitals, to not experience sexual feelings, to masturbate, to want to watch porn and so on. In all of these cases, their distress has been underpinned by not having trusted adults to talk to and a lack of information about their stage of development.

Adolescents have the right to be informed, to be protected and to protect themselves. The United Nations Convention on the Rights of the Child includes the rights of young people to education. If we define education as meaningful, age-appropriate information to guide a young person's development, information about relationships and sexuality is highly relevant to fulfilling this right. Another important right is 'to be protected'. Young people should be protected against any physical and mental harm, including sexual harm, and they also have the right to protect themselves against harm as a result of unwilling or unprotected sexual behaviour such as sexual harassment, sexual abuse, sexual bullying, unplanned pregnancy and sexually transmitted infections. To know how to protect themselves as well as their partner, comprehensive sexuality education is key.

So, discussing sexuality at home is important with several benefits for young people, and in this book we will give you the tools to do this. While school-based relationships and sexuality education is also vital, young people need additional support and guidance in this aspect of their development. Both formal (e.g. school-based) and informal (e.g. home-based, social media etc.) relationships and sexuality education are needed and should be complementary, but this is often not the case.

Challenge 5: Social media

In 2019 more than 90% of teenagers in the USA, UK and Australia had their own smartphone[8] with more than 70% of 15–24 year olds having access to the internet and social media. While the internet is a great source of knowledge and a way of connecting with or making new friends, adults are often concerned about young people's use of the internet because of its 'sexualization'.[9]

There is no denying that the use of digital media has had a huge impact on the knowledge, attitudes and behaviours of adolescents related to sexuality. However, the exact impact is difficult to measure.[10] What we do know is that young people enjoy using digital spaces and will continue to do so. We also know that the potential for the internet to promote diverse understandings is incredible, but at the same time the lack of quality assurance mechanisms means that information sources are of variable quality regarding relationships and sexuality education. We therefore see the internet as an opportunity for young people to learn the importance of critical thinking. In the same way that we teach young people to be cautious in blindly accepting tabloid messages, they can learn to critically evaluate what they read and watch online. By doing this, young people become digitally literate.

Although the use of the internet for sexual behaviour is often perceived by adults as risky, it offers lots of opportunities for young people as well. An increasing number of good sexuality education websites for young people are emerging and the use of sexting (sharing sexual images, video clips or messages on the internet) between adolescents is increasing, although percentages vary worldwide.[11] Research shows that most sexting happens with consent and in the privacy of a relationship, with some adolescents considering sexting as a normal part of flirting. Contrary to what many adults believe, in the majority of cases sexting doesn't have any negative consequences.[12] In fact, it has been shown to have several positive outcomes because it allows young people to have explicit discussions about sexuality without the embarrassment of doing so face-to-face. However, sexting without consent and forwarding private pictures to others does happen. Digital literacy and an understanding of consent, respect, equality and kindness can minimize the risk of sexting and we give examples of how these skills and principles can be developed through relationships and sexuality education in Chapters 6–8.

Summary

Throughout this chapter we have discussed several challenges that parents, carers and teachers have shared with us concerning relationships and sexuality education. These challenges don't necessarily need to be negative though, instead they can become opportunities for meaningful discussions and learning. The key messages addressed were:

- The term sex education refers to just one aspect of sexuality; we therefore promote the term sexuality education.

- Sexuality education should support the development of specific competencies of young people and the content should be based on the needs of the young people themselves.

- Being aware of your values and how they can influence your motives and the messages you convey in relationships and sexuality education makes it easier to distinguish between factual information and personal opinion.

- Discussing relationships and sexuality at home can benefit your relationship with your teenager. It shows them that it's safe to ask questions at home about these issues.

- Social media, if used safely, can present positive opportunities for young people to connect with others and to find valuable information based on their specific needs.

- Digital literacy and critical thinking are important skills for young people to be able to distinguish between the varying levels of quality of information offered on the internet.

Returning to the questions from young people that we set out at the beginning of this chapter, we hope that in reading it you may now have some thoughts regarding what could have been done differently to make these young people's relationships and sexuality education more meaningful and relatable to their everyday lives. In the next chapter we share some ideas about communicating with young people about relationships and sexuality.

Chapter 3

Communicating with adolescents about sex and sexuality

Over the years, we have found that many parents want to help their teenagers learn about relationships and sexuality, but they haven't been sure how to. They haven't been able to find the right words and the right moments to talk about love, trust, respect, boundaries, bodies, masturbation, orgasm, sexual intercourse and so on. Because of these challenges, many adults repeatedly postpone and delay these conversations until they talk themselves out of it completely. They may think that it's too embarrassing or difficult or that young people probably know all they need to know through school, friends or the internet. In other words, many adults struggle with the 'how' and 'when' of sexuality conversations.

As parents and professionals, we know that these kinds of conversations can sometimes be difficult. We've stumbled over our words and found it difficult to engage the resistant teenager too. So, in this chapter, we share our tricks and tips along with those of educators internationally.

Let's start by looking at what we mean by 'communicating'.

Talking or communicating?

Parents and carers sometimes think that one talk, or 'the talk', should be enough to tell a young person everything they need to know about sexuality and after this they assume that the young person will ask if they have any questions. However, this plan falls down in that there is far too much information to be covered by just one 'talk', secondly, relying on a young person to lead the conversation by asking questions rarely works and, finally, the term 'the talk' suggests that the conversation is just one way. So, as you may have guessed, we're not fans of 'the talk'! Instead, we believe that ongoing, stage-appropriate communication that makes use of everyday life to make learning relevant and effective for young people is a much better use of your time and theirs.

Communication is different to 'talking' as it involves listening as well as verbal (with words) and non-verbal communication. People communicate all the time, both with and without words, through their behaviours, gestures, laughs and remarks. Silence is also a means of communication. Even if an adult has said nothing about sexuality to their child throughout their entire life, they will have definitely conveyed several messages. For example when watching a film together, if a sex scene begins, the parent may immediately click away from the scene on the screen. No words will have been said but a clear message will have been conveyed. Every reaction, even no reaction, is a form of communication and conveys a message. If an adult laughs at homophobic behaviour in a film, they are giving a clear message even though LGBTIQ+ issues haven't been discussed. When schools or parents don't provide any lessons about relationships and sexuality, the message may be interpreted as 'relationships and sexuality shouldn't be discussed', 'this is too embarrassing to discuss', 'sexuality is unimportant' or 'you're too young to understand'. Teenagers are likely to be receptive to such messages and search for answers elsewhere.

It takes time to learn a skill

For adults who are new to communicating about relationships and sexuality with young people and/or live in a cultural context where these kinds of conversations are taboo, we want to be clear that we don't want anyone to feel that they have to use sexual language that they are uncomfortable with. However, we believe that as a minimum adults should enable young people to be able to clearly communicate (with or without words) their boundaries and desires in sexual situations. This is essential because these are the foundations for both giving and obtaining 'consent' for sexual interactions. Just by asking simple questions like 'do you want...?' or 'do you like this...?' and by giving and understanding clear non-verbal signals, young people can check for and respect one another's boundaries. We will discuss consent further in Chapters 5 and 9.

We also believe that anyone who discusses relationships and sexuality with young people has a responsibility to ensure that they talk in an explicit and clear way. For example, if a teacher talks about 'having sex' or 'abstinence' without clearly explaining what these terms mean, there's great scope for confusion. For example, does abstinence refer to kissing, touching each other's genitals, oral or anal sex, touching yourself... what does it mean? Likewise, what is sex? Does it refer only to vaginal penetration with a penis, or perhaps with a finger or something else, does it include oral penetration, does it have to be accompanied by an orgasm...? These are all questions that young people can ask.

There is much ambiguity regarding the meaning of sexual language due to a lack of clear definitions. In Chapter 5 we elaborate more on what terms like virginity, sexual intercourse and other sexual behaviours are commonly held to mean. However, a really important point to make in this chapter is that in order to understand one another, it's essential that you clarify what you mean by any terms that you use with young people when discussing relationships and sexuality.

Communication by role modelling

Behaviour is another form of communication. Children and young people learn by observing and copying others who they admire, love or appreciate. For young children, parents and carers are their main role models, and when they grow up, other adults become their role models as well as peers. Although the peer group becomes extremely important during adolescence, don't underestimate your impact as a role model for adolescents. If an adult is admired or loved by a young person, they can have a huge impact on them.

Role models send important messages about relationships and sexuality through their behaviours and words. Young people use role models to help them develop their self-identity. Questions like 'Who am I?' or 'Who would I like to be like?' become central at this stage with almost every act or behaviour centred around these questions in the search for identity. Role models play an enormous part in this process and may influence the young person's decision making, both positively and negatively.[1] Role models are diverse and may be people at school or they may be far away and unreachable like movie stars, popular influencers, political leaders or religious leaders. Most young people have more than one role model and they tend to use different role models for different purposes, for example one may be used as a role model for the way the young person wants to look and another may influence their career aspirations.

Parents and carers often worry when one or more of these role models has a negative influence on their child or holds different values to them. We advise you to have frequent chats with your adolescent about what you are worried about. These conversations need to be handled carefully to prevent a negative reaction. We suggest that you show your curiosity and interest rather than fear and objections. Discussing the importance of critical thinking can also be helpful. By trying to understand what's going on in your child's mind, you will gain a better understanding of the situation and be able to gently challenge negative influences.

Our approach to adolescents matters

Adolescents want to be taken seriously. When treated with respect and as an equal, miracles can happen in the adult-adolescent relationship. Unfortunately though, too often adults talk *to* young people instead of *with* them.

How we communicate about sexuality with adolescents not only depends on our own views about sexuality (see Chapter 2), but also on how we perceive young people in general. In our workshops, we find that it's important, particularly for teachers, to reflect on their views of young people as these beliefs can influence the level of motivation to deliver sexuality education as well as the nature of its delivery.[2] You may find it helpful to do this short questionnaire about your perceptions of young people:

Do you think young people are:	Yes	No	Undecided
Difficult?			
Aggressive?			
Risk takers?			
Unable to take wise decisions?			
Superficial?			
Followers of others?			
Impulsive?			
Disobedient?			
Selfish?			
Not independent enough?			

If the majority of your answers were yes, you have quite negative perceptions of young people and you might want to consider how these opinions translate to your ideas about young people's sexual development. You might, for example, think that young people aren't capable of making their own decisions about their sexual health, or that their tendency for risk taking will become a challenge once they become sexually active. Thinking that young people aren't yet your equivalent in relation to sexuality might also (negatively) shape your approach to teenagers as they begin to experiment sexually.

The American researcher Amy Schalet[3] published a famous study about how US and Dutch parents approach adolescents' sexuality. Her findings demonstrated that the two cultures handled first sexual relationships amongst adolescents completely differently. She named the research publication and subsequently her book 'Not under my roof' which aptly summarized the views of US parents regarding teenage sexual relationships. These attitudes contrasted with the Dutch parents who were more willing to allow their adolescents' sexual partners to stay in their home overnight. She also used contrasting terms 'dramatizing versus normalizing' to illustrate the attitude of parents from the two cultures towards adolescent sexual development.

In addition to dramatizing the sexual development and sexual behaviours of young people, some adults feel that they need to control adolescents in order to protect them. Controlling behaviours can be a consequence of fear. In this case, fear is often linked to concerns that the young person's behaviour might lead to problems and dangerous situations, or that teenagers are too young for sexual relationships. While these concerns generally come from a well-intended desire to protect young people, such assumptions may lead to adults preventing adolescents from having intimate relationships, which could deprive the young person of an opportunity to learn how to set their own boundaries and develop their autonomy. In addition, controlling behaviours like these can also lead to low self-confidence because decisions aren't taken by the adolescent but by the parent or carer. Setting limits and boundaries for young people is appropriate, but finding a balance between a healthy level of control and too much control, between protection and too much protection, is a must when educating adolescents.

It is the task of sexuality educators, regardless of whether they have an informal or professional role, to discuss the possible consequences of sexual behaviours with young people and to help them develop strategies which minimize the associated risks. Equally though it's important to discuss how young people can make sexual situations pleasurable for themselves and their partner(s). For some, this may mean waiting to have sex for a while or until they are married, for others it may mean that they will wait to have sex until they are in love and for other young people sexual attraction may be enough. The point here is that each young person will have differing perspectives which they need to work out. This is why communicating about relationships and sexuality, giving different perspectives, teaching young people how to critically consider other points of view and discussing the possible consequences of decisions are such important aspects in communicating about relationships and sexuality. Through such discussions young people can develop their ability to take decisions related to their sexual lives.

Sexuality education for young people can, in some ways, be compared to learning to drive a car or a motorbike or going to a music festival for the first time. It's something to look forward to and be excited about. However, as an adult you know that exciting 'firsts' can also include risks and that being unaware of these risks or not knowing how to avoid and/or protect yourself against them can ruin the experience. This is exactly what you can do in comprehensive sexuality education. You can respectfully acknowledge a young person's excitement regarding their sexual feelings, desires or first sexual encounter, but you can also give them the information they need to be protected.

If accepting young people's sexuality is new to you, it's likely that you'll need to adjust your approach and style of communication. Acknowledging the young person's sexual development and sexual feelings is the first step, but this needs to be followed by communicating with them in such a way that the adolescent feels appreciated and safe.[4] Sexuality education is a balance between giving levels of freedom and independence on the one hand and expecting the young person to take responsibility and sticking to agreed boundaries on the other. Likewise, it's a careful balance between showing interest but not too much as young people need their privacy, between giving guidance but not too much as they need to learn from their own mistakes, between listening without judgement and sharing opinions and allowing them to develop their own and, finally, between giving correct factual information and introducing values. Adolescence is a bumpy road, and educating an adolescent is inevitably bumpy too!

Communicating about sexuality in a positive way

As we explained in the Introduction, we support and promote positive sexuality education. Positive sexuality education places an emphasis on the pleasurable side of sexuality. It positions sexuality as something that is human and normal and that should be pleasurable and comfortable for anyone, regardless of age, gender and type of relationship. Sexuality is a positive and powerful force in human life and in many relationships it's the foundation of a pleasurable interaction. This doesn't mean that sex (as in sexual behaviour) is always a natural consequence of a trusting and intimate relationship though. Love, appreciation, kindness, respect and equality can all be expressed in other ways instead of sexual behaviour. Adolescents need to know that sexual behaviour can be an important aspect of a relationship, but it doesn't always have to be.

Instead of the emphasis being placed on how to avoid or prevent problems like unplanned pregnancies, sexually transmitted infections, sexual harassment or abuse, a positive approach places the emphasis on how to make a relationship a comfortable and pleasant one, with or without sexual behaviour. Safety, equality and consent are promoted as an integral part of relationships. If there is sexual behaviour, it should be safe, equal and consensual, but equally if there is no sexual behaviour, these qualities can keep the relationship comfortable too. Other qualities within a relationship such as trust, love, honesty, humour, shared values and being able to 'give and take' can make sexuality and relationships pleasurable, but this is highly personal to the individual. Relationships and sexuality education should help young people work out what matters to them in relationships and how to share and discuss this with a potential partner(s). To be able to do this, a certain level of empathy is needed in the adolescent. Listening, observing and checking their partner's thoughts and feelings is something that young people can learn and that they will benefit from as it is key to developing positive sexual relationships.

A positive approach also includes supporting young people when things go wrong. If an adolescent has been sexually harassed or if they think they are pregnant or have a sexually transmitted infection, it's important for educators to stand back from the situation and avoid making judgements. Far too often we see 'victim-blaming', especially towards adolescents. For example, girls are 'slut-shamed' when having participated in sexting, and if a girl has been harassed late at night she's often blamed for being out late and for the way she chose to dress. Victims should never be blamed. To harass someone because of how they look or because they choose to go out at night is wrong. This may seem obvious but what may be less obvious is how we consider 'adolescent perpetrators'. Our professional experience of working with this group suggests that sometimes young perpetrators don't know that what they are doing or have done is wrong because they have grown up in environments where they have learned that it's 'normal' to force another to have sex or to go further when someone says 'no'. So, in many ways some young perpetrators are victims themselves. Indeed, we have found that this group of young people highlight further the need for comprehensive sexuality education for all.

Tips and tricks for communicating about relationships and sexuality

As we've acknowledged, talking about relationships and sexuality with teenagers isn't always easy but below we've shared some suggestions from educators around the world as to how you can make it easier and more effective:

Teachable moments

For many parents and carers, choosing the right moment to start a conversation about sexual issues is one of the things they find most difficult. Teachers have fewer difficulties because most lessons are planned. Judging the right moment for parents and carers is tricky, and sometimes, even when the timing seems perfect, it's not the right moment for the teenager because they've got homework to do, they're expecting a video call, they need to go to hockey or they just aren't in the right mood to talk. If that's the case, just let the moment pass and wait for another time.

Mealtimes are a great time to talk. Even if joint meals aren't common in your household, we encourage parents and carers to try to ensure that the household comes together and talks over a meal at least once a day around a table. Consider this as quality time with your children. Sharing a meal together gives everyone the opportunity to relax, listen to each other and share their daily experiences. It's a great time to have discussions, provide support and enjoy each other's company.

Other situations which many parents and carers find useful

are those in which you're doing something else together, like cooking, washing the dishes, walking or driving. Any of these kinds of situations is good as the young person can walk away or focus on something else if they don't want to continue. Sitting in front of each other can be too direct and can make a teenager uncomfortable. Whatever the nature of the teachable moment, be sensitive to how long the adolescent might want to talk for. Sometimes a short conversation that is revisited frequently can be more effective than a long discussion which might become boring for the teenager.

Talk about others

Teenagers can easily feel attacked or accused when an adult asks direct questions about them. Questions like 'Do you ever masturbate?' or 'Have you had sex?' could be too direct and perceived as offensive, meaning that an honest answer will be unlikely. A strategy we sometimes use is to ask questions or talk about others as a prompt to ask a teenager what their opinions are. For example: 'I heard that one of the older girls at school is pregnant, I think she's 17. How do you think she'll cope?'; after a while you could ask other questions like 'Do you think 17's a good age to get pregnant?' and 'If the pregnancy wasn't planned, how could they have avoided it?'

Use a current situation

This is similar to the tip above but it uses current news items, stories in newspapers, movies or family news to start the conversation. Watching a movie or TV series together can be great for opening up communication. The best way to start this kind of conversation is by asking a general question like: 'What do you think of them calling a girl a bitch?' or 'Why did they break up, was he mad at him?' General questions are less threatening than specific questions which focus on the young person, but you may find that opening the conversation up in this way will allow you to gradually move from the general to the specific.

Choosing your words

Talking to a teenager about sexuality demands a carefully chosen vocabulary. Using words which are too complex or too scientific can sound old fashioned and boring for a teenager. But using the slang that teenagers use with peers can seem forced and uncomfortable. Depending on the age and developmental level of the adolescent, you may find it helpful to use accurate language interspersed with the young person's language to make the discussion clearer. Most importantly though, be explicit and clear. If you use the word 'sex' or 'the first time', make sure that you both agree what you mean by it and so on (see Chapter 5).

Just listen

Sometimes it works well if you don't immediately react or suggest a solution as part of a conversation. Sometimes a young person doesn't want to hear solutions, they just want to tell their story and share their feelings. That's all. All they want from you is that you listen and empathize. Nodding, saying 'uh huh...' or 'I see...', might be all you need to say.

Label emotions

When having a conversation about sexual issues, emotions are likely to come up. Try not to ignore these emotions but give space and time to them. Label them and use the emotion in your communication. Examples of emotions that may arise include happiness, pride, relief, jealousy, hurt...

'I' messages

Every communication expert will tell you how important it is to use 'I' sentences to avoid accusatory or blaming conversations. Take these two examples: 'You always make a mess of the kitchen when you come home' as opposed to 'I cleaned the kitchen just before you came home and it makes me frustrated when I see that it needs to be cleaned again just five minutes later. Could you put everything away please so that it looks like it did before?' Can you see that the second example is less accusatory and is less likely to make the adolescent feel attacked and defensive? An 'I' statement makes a person responsible for their own thoughts and feelings rather than attributing them, sometimes falsely or unfairly, to someone else.

The art of negotiation

When young people want to push the limits, a common response by adults is to come down hard and set the limits for them. Phrases like 'You're not going out dressed like that!' and 'You're not to see her again!', among others, are common examples of parents and carers doing this, but the problem is that some adolescents want to break rules. Too many rules or rules that are too strict can be interpreted by a teenager as a lack of trust and a lack of respect for them as emerging adults, which can be damaging to relationships.

So rather than imposing rules you need to master the art of negotiation! For example, rather than dictating what time you expect your teenager to come home from a party, ask them what time they think is reasonable. If you don't agree, negotiate with them until you reach a compromise that's acceptable to the two of you. By doing this you're involving the young person in the decision-making process and they're more likely to understand your point of view. Negotiation doesn't mean that you have to be permissive though; it's important for the adolescent to understand that although you're willing to negotiate and listen to their perspective you will have the final say.

Bringing in your own experiences

Among sexuality educators there is no real agreement as to whether to share personal experiences in sexuality lessons or not. Some do and others don't. It depends upon the situation and the individual's willingness. Usually, it's more comfortable to do so in the private setting of the family in response to an adolescent asking direct questions about their parents' or carers' previous experiences. But it's also OK if the parent decides not to share their personal experiences, it's up to them. There's no right or wrong.

However, to share your own experiences in the absence of any questions from a young person isn't always a good idea. They may see your experiences as irrelevant as you were young during a different era. Using your past to support your argument might have an undesired effect, for example a likely response to you saying 'When I was your age, I wasn't allowed to have a girlfriend, so don't think your girlfriend can sleep here' may be 'But in your time everything was different, things are completely different now!' And they're right.

Stay positive and use humour

Sexual conversations can be uncomfortable, but by using humour and positivity the situation can be more relaxed. These kinds of conversations don't need to be too serious as sexuality is, after all, something normal and human. In the classroom, using fun games, quizzes and debates can make the atmosphere lighter for everyone, as we discuss in Chapters 6, 7 and 8.

Summary

In this chapter we have discussed the 'how' of communicating about relationships and sexuality with young people. Let's give young people the message that it's OK to talk about these things. Through communication it is possible to resolve misunderstandings, provide support and help young people develop their personal opinions and values. Through communication we can also become more connected with each other.

Some key messages we gave in this chapter were:

- Communication is much more than only talking. It includes listening and sending verbal and non-verbal messages.

- When communicating about sexuality with young people, one needs to be explicit and clear. When sharing unclear or confusing messages, young people could make their own interpretation which may not be in line with what you mean.

- Young people also learn about sexuality from watching, copying and interpreting behaviours of others outside the inner family circle. If you are not happy with some of these new role models, discuss the importance of critical thinking with your adolescent.

- Young people want to be taken seriously. When you communicate, don't just talk *to* them, talk *with* them, too.

- In your approach, it's important to find a balance between controlling and guiding, protecting and supporting to become independent.

- It is very important to be positive in your communication about sexuality. Giving warnings and restrictions will not be helpful. They create fear or incredulity. It is more effective to discuss how to make sexuality and sexual relations pleasurable and enjoyable. Safety and consent are topics which should be included.

- When searching for the right moment to start a conversation about sexuality, make use of teachable moments.

However, although the tips that have been shared in this chapter can contribute to effective communication with adolescents, there's no guarantee that they will work. An understanding of why adolescents behave in the way they do is also needed, and this will be explored in the next chapter where we discuss the physical and mental changes that occur during adolescence and how these can influence young people's mood, self-concept, relationships and sexual development.

Chapter 4

Towards a better understanding of our teenagers

BODY, BRAINS AND SEX

'I don't want to be a teenager, I'm already tired of feeling so much. Life was so much easier when I was young. But I can't wait to be grown up and earn money and go to bed as late as I want.'

(12 year old talking to his dad)

Puberty can be a rollercoaster for many young people, with huge changes occurring in their brains and bodies as well as socially and sexually. As adults, our role is to help our teenagers navigate their way through what sometimes feel like heavy storms towards calmer water.

One way of doing this is to understand the physical and mental changes that occur during puberty and adolescence. Increasing hormone production is usually the start of many changes. Physical changes are the easiest to spot but changes within the brain are just as significant. Development of different parts of the brain occurs at a different rate to the outward physical changes but these have a huge impact on the mental state of adolescents. We will discuss the role of hormones throughout this chapter, along with the accompanying physical and mental changes. We will also discuss the effect of hormones on young people's sexual feelings and behaviours as well as the biopsychosocial aspect of sexual development which demonstrates how sexual feelings and behaviours are also affected by physical and brain development.

Before making a start we want to emphasize that every adolescent is unique and will develop in an individual way. Some will develop faster and sooner than others, whereas other young people may develop more slowly and later, but each adolescent will experience most of the changes we describe in their own time. The road they follow will be individual but the end result will be more or less the same for the majority: the emergence of an autonomous young adult.

Hormones are the trigger

In most children when they are growing up in primary school, small amounts of hormones are released into their bodies, but as soon as they reach a specific combination of height and weight, the hypothalamus of the brain usually releases a hormone called gonadotropin releasing hormone (GnRH) which stimulates the production of two further hormones from the pituitary gland: luteinizing hormone (LH) and follicle stimulating hormone (FSH). For the majority of children these two hormones act on the testes and ovaries to develop their reproductive functions. FSH and LH also control the levels of hormones produced by the testes and ovaries. One of these hormones, testosterone, is produced by the testes and controls the production of sperm in men. Progesterone and oestrogen are produced by the ovaries and these are instrumental in controlling the maturation and release of an egg during each menstrual cycle. This cascade of hormones also triggers the physical changes which are understood to mean that puberty has started. But inside, at an emotional level, these hormones are also contributing to mood changes, sexual desire and sexual arousal. However, it's important to note that these changes are not only influenced by biological changes, social factors also play a role.

For more information about hormones you may find this website useful: www.yourhormones.info/hormones/gonadotrophin-releasing-hormone.

Help, my body is changing!

In western countries puberty usually begins somewhere between 7 and 13 years of age in girls and between 9 and 15 years in boys. But as we have said, there are many individual differences in the start, speed and order of physical changes. In the following discussion we make a distinction between girls' and boys' physical development in puberty. It doesn't mean that people can only be divided into these two separate genders though; we discuss this further later in this chapter.

In girls, the physical changes usually begin with breast development. First the nipples develop and then the tissue around the nipples begins to grow. Breast development can take a long time and each breast can develop at a different speed. Some girls' breast development continues into their 20s. Hair will also grow under the armpits and around the vulva (pubic hair) as well as on the legs and arms. The vulva itself also changes in size and colour (see Chapters 6 and 8) which sometimes causes confusion in adolescent girls because the vulva lips (or labia) are often no longer the same size. The inner lips can become longer than the outer lips or just one of them might. It's also usual for girls to experience an increase in body fat and weight gain. This is normal but some girls find this alarming, particularly if it occurs prior to their growth spurt, and want to start dieting at this young age. In this situation it's important that girls understand that their body will change a lot throughout puberty and will look very different in a couple of years. It's also important to note that dieting can disturb pubertal development, so it's a good idea to check with a family doctor as to whether dieting is appropriate and safe.

Sometime around this stage many girls grow taller very rapidly. While all of these changes are happening, girls may notice that they discharge a small amount of creamy white fluid from their vagina. The onset of this varies significantly from girl to girl but this always comes before their first period, although it may be years or just months before. During this time, girls can also develop acne on their face and sometimes on their back, neck and shoulders. They may also develop body odour. Pimples and a stronger body odour are caused by hormones which stimulate glands to produce oils in addition to sweat. Bacteria breaks down in the sweat under the arms and in the groin area and it is this that produces body odour. The oils in the skin pores can lead to small areas of inflammation when in contact with bacteria, causing pimples and acne.

Around two to two and a half years after the first sign of puberty, most girls experience their first period. Many girls start their periods without having learnt about menstruation and this can be very frightening for them. More information about discussing menstruation with a teenager is provided in Chapter 6. The onset of menstruation marks the end of puberty and its associated rapid physical changes, but it doesn't mean that growth and other physical changes have completely stopped. They will continue but at a slower rate than before.

It is important that boys understand how girls develop and vice versa. In boys the first sign of puberty is the growth of some of the body's extremities: fingers, feet and the penis. As a parent you may no longer see your son naked if he likes his privacy, but if he suddenly needs new shoes every three months you'll know: 'Ahaa... puberty has started!'

Some boys might start puberty with some nipple growth and the development of breasts, but although this is only temporary it can be very embarrassing and confusing for boys. Hair will start to grow on the body and around the penis (pubic hair) and soon he will begin to grow some facial hair. His voice will break and will change to a lower pitch; this also happens to a girl's voice, but the change is more subtle. His muscles will become bigger and stronger and he will also grow taller. Acne and a change of body odour are also common for boys at this stage. As soon as he has his first ejaculation, which is likely to be somewhere between 12 and 15 years of age, the growth spurt will stop and his physical changes will continue at a slower speed.

In girls, their first period tends not to go unnoticed because they may need some help. But a boy's first ejaculation frequently happens with nobody else knowing because it might occur during sleep. If a boy isn't prepared for their first ejaculation and if he doesn't know that it can happen when he is asleep, he might become confused and think that he has wet the bed. In Chapter 6 you will find an example of a conversation between a parent and a child about a boy's first ejaculation.

Gender identity, masculinity and femininity

As we discussed in Chapter 3, identity becomes increasingly important throughout adolescence. Some young people are very clear in their gender awareness and gender expression. They are a boy, a girl, gender fluid, non-binary or whatever they want to be. That's what they are and that's fine for them. For others though it might not be so clear, and although they desperately want to identify as a certain gender, they may feel confused and anxious because they don't feel like a boy or a girl or how they feel doesn't match their biological sex by birth. This confusion can be very painful because of the emphasis adolescents place on their identity. Who they are, what others think of them and how they should behave are all questions related to this search for identity, and questions around gender can be central to this search.

Some adolescents also feel uncomfortable about their bodies changing. For example, some girls feel ill at ease with the new 'womanliness' of their bodies. For some it is because they don't feel ready to grow up or feel self-conscious, but for others it may be because they are transgender. This may be a transitional phase and they might become more comfortable with the gender assigned to them at birth at some later time or they may not. Others may seem happily cisgender, but later feel differently about their gender identities. Young people's gender identities should be accepted, but it should also be recognized that gender identities can change, particularly during adolescence when bodies, feelings and identities are developing, and no one should be pressured to stick to one particular identity or another. (See Chapter 7, topic 9, for more on gender identity.)

Even today, perceptions of being a boy/man or a girl/woman often conform to stereotypical expectations regarding masculinity or femininity. Although norms around gender expression can differ from one context to another, not conforming to certain dress codes including the colours of clothes and other gendered behaviours can lead to bullying or isolation. For this reason we advocate that an integral part of relationships and sexuality education should include ongoing discussions with young people which question the need to adhere to these norms. Critical thinking is one of the goals of relationships and sexuality education, and encouraging teenagers to reflect and question stereotypical beliefs regarding masculinity and femininity should be a part of their education. A useful tool to use with adolescents in explaining the differences and similarities between concepts like gender expression, biological sex, gender identity and sexual orientation is the 'Genderbread Person' (see www.genderbread.org). We will explain this tool in more detail in the next chapter.

Brain development and its influence on mental and emotional development

The brain is an integral part of the body. Its development is linked to young people's psychological and social functioning as well as their behaviour. Some people refer to this as 'the teenage mind', but for clarity we have used the term 'brain', while acknowledging that social factors also have a role in this aspect of adolescent development.

From around the age of 10 to 25 years, the developing brain directs mood, preferences, decisions and behaviours. The order of brain development is consistent across all adolescents, but the speed of development is highly variable. In addition to initiating sexual development, hormones trigger the development and maturation of the brain. In childhood, brain development is focused on the parts of the brain which are especially related to motor and language development. During adolescence the frontal part of the brain, the prefrontal cortex, develops significantly and this is responsible for a wide variety of functions[1] including: mentally playing with ideas, coping with unanticipated challenges, staying focused, predicting the consequences of actions and anticipating events in the environment.

These functions are necessary in order to function independently and optimally in a social setting.[2] They are also integral to the development of a teenager's identity. The development of these specific functions is affected not only by biological but also by environmental factors,[3] so parents, carers, teachers and other professionals can support an adolescent's development in this regard by encouraging them to socialize with peers and to experiment with different social experiences so that they can use their brain functions and skills in different situations.

Core functions for which the prefrontal cortex is responsible include:[4]

- inhibition or self-control, e.g. resisting temptations or resisting acting impulsively

- cognitive flexibility, e.g. thinking 'outside-of-the-box', seeing something from different perspectives and quickly adapting to changing circumstances

- being able to work according to a plan, curiosity, being able to consider behavioural alternatives including the ability to make risk assessments

- making decisions based on an overview of consequences and correct risk assessment

- self-reflection and self-insight

- social monitoring, which is related to empathy and enables the adolescent to recognize, understand and even feel what is happening with others.

To develop these functions takes many years and the adolescent not only needs the guidance and coaching of adults, they also need experiences in which they can practise these skills, sometimes using trial and error. Contrary to what many think, brain development continues well after puberty and goes beyond the years spent in secondary school and even the legal age of adulthood. The prefrontal cortex doesn't finish developing until around the age of 25 and its development is dependent upon a combination of biopsychosocial factors, including sex hormones, physical changes and the adolescent's close social environment. It is a complex network of interactions, some positive, others negative, but with a long-term impact on the adolescent's life. This is why adolescence should be considered not just as a period in between childhood and adulthood, or as a transitional stage, but as an important separate stage in life, full of challenges and opportunities.

Developing autonomy

Growing up involves a gradual process of becoming independent from others, especially adults. Children make small steps towards independence as soon as they learn to talk and walk, but during adolescence this process accelerates. Autonomy is more than just developing independence though; it is also concerned with knowing and trusting yourself, knowing what you are capable of, knowing your values and knowing your limits.

Autonomy is also related to self-identity. Every day, adolescents become increasingly self-aware through the feedback that they get from others in response to what they do and say. A warm and supportive environment can make a huge difference to the development of the adolescent's self-identity. But this environment doesn't have to be limited to the family setting – anyone who is emotionally close to and appreciated by the young person can create this kind of supportive context for a young person. Being judged, bullied or humiliated can even be compensated for through these kinds of supportive environments. Providing support to a young person in how to become self-confident and independent, showing belief in their skills despite regular failures and enabling them to deal with challenges is part of our task as adults in helping adolescents develop autonomy. This can be a bumpy journey but even experiences that are perceived as failures are helpful in prompting self-reflection and further enabling young people to develop their self-identity and autonomy.

Developing empathy

By encouraging a teenager to reflect on their emotions and think about the emotions that might underpin their behaviour, young people learn to become more empathetic. As we explained in our first book, the development of empathy starts early in life but during adolescence more nuances of the complex concept of empathy are learned. By being able to recognize and label their own emotions, which is a first step in building empathy, an adolescent has the foundations for observing and recognizing emotions in others, which is the second step in developing empathy.

However, to recognize emotions in other people, development of the prefrontal cortex is needed. Research shows that adults are better at judging others' emotions and body language than adolescents because the prefrontal cortex is not yet fully developed in young people. Understanding this can be enormously helpful as it explains why some adolescents struggle with understanding the perspective of others.

This is also highly relevant to sexuality education, as the whole topic of 'consent' is closely related to the ability to take another's perspective. Many teenagers aren't yet able to completely do this. However, the good news is that you can help young people in developing empathy and thus learn how to apply principles of consent. We elaborate more on how you can do this in the following chapters, but here are some brief ideas for now:

- Be a role model in your own social behaviour and interactions.

- Discuss and label your own emotions.

- Give young people feedback about what you see and hear in their behaviours and the emotion behind it.

- Support young people in reflecting on other people's feelings and behaviours by asking questions like: *'What do you think she's feeling?'* or *'What do you think he meant by doing that?'*

- Discuss what prejudices mean and what the consequences of prejudices can be.

- Discuss how it can be tricky to accurately guess what someone means by their behaviour.

Understanding the need for consent in intimate and romantic relationships and being able to judge whether consent has been given is contingent on the development of empathy. Only then can consent become an integral part of pleasurable, equal and enjoyable relationships. We will come back to consent in Chapters 5–9.

Summary

In this chapter we have given an overview of the physical, mental and emotional changes that occur during puberty and adolescence. Here are some key messages from this chapter:

- Puberty is only a short part of the long road called adolescence.

- Puberty triggers the production of sex hormones, which bring about rapid physical changes. These hormones also trigger the development of brain structures which, in turn, have a huge impact on the adolescent's behaviour and emotions.

- Brain development can continue up to the mid-20s.

- Adolescence should be considered an independent and separate part of human development. Adolescents can, therefore, be considered a 'work in progress' with great potential.

- Biological as well as environmental influences play a complementary role in shaping adolescent identity.

- The social environment of the teenager and their cultural context have a significant impact on the building of autonomy and self-identity. This means that adults can have a positive impact by giving support, accepting the young person without judgement, encouraging them to express their thoughts, helping them to label their emotions and by showing empathy.

Having considered how brain development affects young people's mental and emotional development, in the next chapter we consider its impact on sexual development and sexual behaviour.

Chapter 5

The sexual lives of adolescents

In this chapter we'll look at the impact of the biopsychosocial context of adolescent sexual behaviours and sexual relationships. We'll use research from the Netherlands[1] as a framework because the Netherlands has a unique set of data about the sexuality of 12 to 25 year olds which has been collected every five years since 1995. The data collected in these national surveys takes into account all young people, with different backgrounds, genders and sexual orientation. While we appreciate that this book will be read all over the world by readers who may live in less progressive contexts than the Netherlands, this dataset is extremely useful in providing a unique insight into this under-researched field. Where research is available from other countries we will also draw on this. But first, let's have a look at the connection between brain development and sexual behaviour during adolescence.

What does brain development have to do with sexual development?

Below we have summarized how the milestones in physical and brain development, discussed in the previous chapters, impact upon young people's sexual behaviour. In the following tables we have drawn from research presented in a Dutch book, *Het tienerbrein* by Professor Jelle Jolles,[2] to explain this relationship. Remember, although the tables below are based on ages, stages of development will differ from one young person to another and can differ significantly depending on the nature of the environment in which the adolescent grows up. So these are only intended as a guide. Another important point to make clear is that we do not suggest a causal relationship between physical/brain development and the sexual behaviours of adolescents. However, we believe that there is an interaction between physical/brain development, social factors and sexual development. We have aimed to summarize some of these interactions in the following tables.

12–13 years of age: Early adolescence

Milestones in physical development and brain development	Sexual development
Physical changes	Increased focus on how they look.
Sexual feelings	Need for masturbation, falling in love.
Interest in adult sexuality	Curious to know more about sex, sexuality and adult sexual behaviour and to watch porn.
Thinking in a concrete way	Ideas about what is 'acceptable' or perceived as 'normal' may be quite rigid.
Focus on short-term consequences	Will choose the option that will give immediate satisfaction, for example texting someone they have a crush on instead of finishing homework.
Spontaneous behaviour, difficulty inhibiting behaviour	Acting before thinking (for example: sharing personal data online with strangers, sending nude pics).
Sensation seeking	Inclined to engage in situations which give immediate thrills, for example watching porn with peers, use of alcohol/drugs with peers. Vulnerable to peer pressure.

Strong emotions	Can become highly excited when love is reciprocated and deeply depressed if not.
Limited self-reflection	Mistakes are not always considered their fault. For example when asked why they distributed nude pics of a classmate: 'It's her fault that they're on my phone, she shouldn't have sent them to me.'
Difficulty recognizing emotions in others	Finds it difficult to imagine what the other is thinking or wanting in a relationship. Has difficulty in understanding the long-term impact of bullying/sexting.

14–15 years of age: Mid-adolescence

Milestones in physical development and brain development	Sexual development
Most girls will have finished puberty; most boys will have experienced first ejaculation	Most girls' bodies are mature and many want to emphasize their femininity in how they look. 'Looking sexy' means being attractive, it's not necessarily about attracting others. Boys become aware of the link between ejaculation and sexual feelings. Masturbation increases in boys, not (yet) in girls (see Chapter 7, topic 4, for discussion about girls and masturbation).
Is able to plan simple tasks	Able to discuss/reflect on short-term steps in new relationships.
Long-term choices or decisions are still difficult to make	May need support in making decisions about sexual relationships and use of contraception.
Thrill-seeking	Sensations and thrills give an immediate and positive reward. In CSE there needs to be a specific focus on long-term consequences of behaviours.
Tendency to be impulsive	Prefers immediate satisfaction without being aware of negative long-term consequences. Needs help in judging long-term consequences.
Strong emotions	Needs support in managing negative emotions.

cont.

Milestones in physical development and brain development	Sexual development
Peer group becomes very important	Needs approval from peer group, vulnerable to peer pressure, values are developed based on what the peer group says or values. Rules and values of peers will have significant impact upon sexual behaviours, interacting with other genders and views on sexual minorities. However, values of close adults are still important.
Decision-making skills not yet fully developed	Can make a decision, but decisions are often sudden and spontaneous and not always based on accurate information. This plays a role in decisions related to sexual behaviour, particularly safe sexual relationships and consensual relationships.

16+: Late adolescence

Milestones in physical development and brain development	Sexual development
Most boys have finished puberty and are taller than girls of same age; boys and girls are now physically ready to reproduce	When starting sexual relationships, awareness of the possibility of pregnancy and how to prevent it is important.
Better at planning, even for complex tasks; able to make complex choices, for the short, mid- and long term	Able to plan and make well-informed decisions related to long-term relationships and long-term consequences of sexual behaviour such as parenthood and protecting against this, as long as adults provide some support.
Less likely to take sudden and spontaneous decisions but still need immediate rewards	Can still be tempted by immediate rewards from spontaneous decisions, but more aware of possible negative consequences and able to inhibit spontaneous behaviours. For example, the adolescent will now understand that studying for an upcoming exam is a better idea than talking for hours with a new partner.

Better at planning, prioritizing, judging own intentions and evaluating own choices	Able to reflect on own choice: 'That one-night stand wasn't a wise decision.'
More resistant to social pressures	'All my friends want to wait to have sex until they are older, but I am curious and don't want to wait.'
Judgements, behaviours and values are still dependent on the peer group's approval	'I don't like porn, but my friends will think I'm weird if I don't watch it with them.'
Able to recognize and label complex emotions in others	'I can see you're upset by that dick-pic, they shouldn't have done that.'
Able to feel the perspective of others	'He must feel terrible that she humiliated him like that.' Adults can now promote compassionate empathy through meaningful discussion.
Needs opportunities to experiment	Adults need to give teenagers the opportunity to experiment with spontaneous behaviours by encouraging the young person to make their own decisions and offering them support in reducing potential negative consequences. For example: 'If you've decided to have sex and you've thought through the consequences, here's a packet of condoms. Make sure you use them when the time is right!'
Needs support, guidance and a positive environment	'You want your boyfriend to stay over? I know you've thought it through. Invite him over. Condoms are in the bathroom.'

As you can see in these tables, the development of the prefrontal cortex coincides with the development of behaviour and emotions which are closely linked to relationships and sexuality. However, brain development shouldn't be used as an excuse for limiting or prohibiting young people to explore and experiment with their sexual feelings. Nor should brain development be used to imply that all adolescents follow the same pattern of social and emotional development. The specific context in which a child grows up is likely to interact with biological and mental changes during adolescence, meaning that each young person will experience adolescence in their own unique way. In giving relationships and sexuality education to adolescents it would be wise to keep this in mind.

What do we know about the development of adolescent sexual behaviours?

In many western European societies heterosexual adolescents start their 'sexual career' (sexual behaviours in intimate relationships) in slow steps in a certain order. Many non-hetero young people report having different experiences during adolescence and we will come back to this later in this section.

According to Dutch research,[3] heterosexual young people report that they generally fall in love or feel attracted to someone before engaging in any physical behaviour. They may begin to be physically close to the other person, and may kiss on the lips and progress to kissing inside the mouth (French kissing). Later they may touch the breasts and genitals over clothes, progressing to touching each other under clothing, undressing themselves and lying naked next to each other, touching each other's genitals and masturbating each other to orgasm (manual sexual behaviour). This may progress to oral sex where they touch the other's genitals with the mouth and lick and suck the other's genitals until orgasm, sexual intercourse which involves the penis entering the vagina towards orgasm, and, sometimes, anal sex, where the penis enters the anus to orgasm. In many heterosexual adolescent sexual interactions, the orgasm is on the part of the boys and less often in the girls.[4] This gender gap is called 'the orgasm gap'.[5] We will come back to this in Chapter 7 because it has implications for the content of relationships and sexuality education.

The behaviours described above come from the Dutch national survey[6] which we outlined earlier. According to the Dutch research, these steps often happen in this order but not always. The steps may be taken over several years in different encounters with some time in between each encounter and perhaps with different partners, or they may all occur in one evening. Dutch researchers[7] describe this process as the step-wise sexual development of young people in the Netherlands. From the first French kiss to first sexual intercourse takes around two and a half to three years on average for Dutch young people. Unfortunately, there is a lack of research beyond the Netherlands which has explored whether the stepwise approach to sexual development applies to young people internationally; our professional experience suggests that in some places it does, but this may not be uniform.

We advocate this approach to sexual development because by going through these steps, in their own time, young people are able to discover their personal sexual wishes and desires, their boundaries and their limits. They are also better able to judge what they want next, and are less vulnerable to acquiescing to pressure, crossing their personal boundaries and engaging in risky sexual behaviours.[8]

In several western countries it appears that the median age at which young people engage in different types of sexual behaviour has increased.[9] For example in the USA between 2013 and 2017 there was a decline in the proportion of high school students who had had sexual intercourse.[10] Likewise, in the UK, Australia and other western countries a decline in interactional sexual behaviour has been reported.[11] The reasons for this are complex and varied but one factor appears to relate to the increased use of social media among young people. Making contact and flirting happens more online than in real life today, with young people finding it easier to make this step online and sometimes finding it more difficult to meet offline.[12]

Many parents and carers have questions regarding masturbation. With regards to when young people start to masturbate and how common it is, there are significant gender differences. Boys start earlier and masturbate more than girls. In the Dutch research,[13] about 35% of the boys between 12 and 14 years of age reported having experience with masturbation, compared to 6% of girls of the same age. During adulthood, this pattern continues with more men than women reporting that they masturbate.[14] The reason we have drawn attention to these gender differences is that masturbating is seen by many sexologists as a useful method for young people to discover their sexual feelings as well as their sexual likes and dislikes. Some experts even argue that learning to masturbate is a precondition for learning to enjoy sexual relationships.[15] If this is the case, adolescent girls who start to masturbate years later than boys, or who never start, may be disadvantaged in discovering their sexuality.[16]

For some people the term 'masturbation' has negative connotations due to values they developed throughout childhood. Some sexologists and sexuality educators have decided to use other, more positive terms instead, like 'sexual self-care', 'self-pleasure' or 'solo-sex'. If this helps young people to have a more positive view on this self-caring behaviour and feel less guilty about it, we certainly encourage the use of alternative words.

Returning now to what we said earlier about stepwise sexual development not relating to all young people, this is especially so among young people who are searching for their sexual identity. The discovery of one's sexual and romantic attraction to people of the same, other or both sexes often occurs in late childhood or during adolescence. With sex hormones being produced in high quantities during puberty, teenagers also experience increasingly intense sexual feelings. Young people discover specific triggers (or 'sexual stimuli') which give them a pleasant and, sometimes, exciting physical sensation centred in their genitals. Sexologists say that boys experience these feelings earlier and more clearly than girls because their physical reaction, i.e. an erect penis, is more easily recognized than the physical signs of arousal for girls (lubrication of the vagina, swollen vulva, faster blood flow, increased heart rate, bigger pupils). Because young people start to experience these sexual feelings in response to certain stimuli, such as seeing a boy or a girl's naked body, a certain sexual gesture given by a male or female or a specific smell, they begin to discover whether they feel more attracted to males, females or both.[17]

If a teenager grows up in a community or cultural context where homosexuality or bisexuality is taboo or rejected, recognizing their own homo-/bisexual feelings can be very difficult, with potential outcomes including denial, rejection, a search for cures and medication, depression and even suicide.[18] At the very least, for some young people, discovering that they are attracted to someone of the same sex or to both can be very confusing if they have grown up in an environment where heterosexuality is the norm. It can be very lonely to feel different to peers who may have begun their (hetero)sexual career. Some young people can even feel abnormal and so they may ignore or deny their sexual feelings, hoping that they will change as they grow older. Or they may 'try' to be heterosexual and date and have sex, to see whether their true sexual feelings will disappear.

Acceptance of one's sexual orientation and sexual identity

is easier in an environment which is open and tolerant towards sexual diversity. To create openness and tolerance, it can be helpful to debunk myths. For example, an individual's sexual orientation isn't learnt nor is it hereditary. There isn't a specific gene for sexual orientation.[19] Children who grow up with only one parent or with two parents of the same sex aren't necessarily going to become gay.[20] There is no proof that negative sexual experiences with the other sex can change someone's sexual orientation. And, importantly, conversion therapy doesn't work and can be harmful for the individual emotionally.[21]

Sexual behaviour and sexual orientation aren't always consistent. If a young person has fallen in love, or has engaged in sexual behaviour with someone of the same sex or feels attracted to someone of the same sex or both sexes, it doesn't necessarily mean that they are gay, lesbian or bisexual. A person may have a preference for sexual behaviours with the same sex but may not feel that their sexual orientation is gay. Likewise, they may have experiences with people of a different sex and not feel they are heterosexual. It's important for young people to understand this because although some will be gay or heterosexual and will know this for sure, for others these experiences are simply part of their journey in figuring out their sexual orientation or sexual identity. This is evident in the Dutch research[22] we mentioned earlier, with around 5% of the 12–18 year old boys and girls having had a sexual experience with someone of the same sex, but only 3% of the boys and 1% of the girls describing themselves as gay, lesbian or bisexual. These data show that sexual orientation during adolescence is fluid with young people increasingly resisting being 'put in a box' or adhering to a fixed label.

A useful way of illustrating the complexity of sexual orientation, sexual attraction and sexual feelings along with gender identity and biological sex is the use of the 'Genderbread Person' (see more explanations and illustrations on www.genderbread. org). As you'll see in the picture below, the Genderbread Person makes a clear distinction between biological sex, gender expression, gender identity and sexual orientation. Although we are aware of the ongoing debates around this tool, it is useful in explaining how the different aspects might be related but don't have to be, and an individual's biological or anatomical sex (i.e. based on the genitals at birth) doesn't determine how they should express their gender, who they should feel attracted to or what they should identify as.

The Genderbread Person v4 *by its pronounced METROsexual.com*

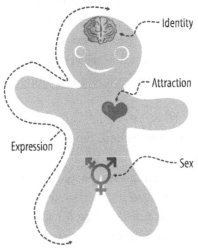

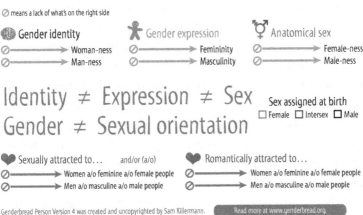

⊘ means a lack of what's on the right side

🧠 **Gender identity**
⊘————————▶ Woman-ness
⊘————————▶ Man-ness

🧍 Gender expression
⊘————————▶ Femininity
⊘————————▶ Masculinity

⚥ Anatomical sex
⊘————————▶ Female-ness
⊘————————▶ Male-ness

Identity ≠ Expression ≠ Sex
Gender ≠ Sexual orientation

Sex assigned at birth
☐ Female ☐ Intersex ☐ Male

💜 Sexually attracted to... and/or (a/o)
⊘————————▶ Women a/o feminine a/o female people
⊘————————▶ Men a/o masculine a/o male people

💜 Romantically attracted to...
⊘————————▶ Women a/o feminine a/o female people
⊘————————▶ Men a/o masculine a/o male people

Genderbread Person Version 4 was created and uncopyrighted by Sam Killermann. 〔 Read more at www.genderbread.org 〕

What about 'the first time'?

Adults often consider the first time a young person has sexual intercourse (or the sexarche) as a significant step towards adulthood, and the significance of 'the first time' can seem greater for them than for the adolescents themselves. Some parents and carers want to protect their children (particularly daughters) from what they perceive to be a too early, unexpected or disappointing first time, to the extent that they prohibit them from sexual experimentation completely. Other parents can be so curious that they expect the young person to share every detail with them afterwards, which can be very uncomfortable for the young person. In the context of developing autonomy, it's better if parents respect this private aspect of their teenager's life and explain that they are there for support if the teenager wants this.

In the Dutch study,[23] in which different adolescent sexual relationships were researched, when asked about their first experience of sexual intercourse, about a third of both boys and girls said it happened unexpectedly. An unexpected first sexual experience can lead to negative feelings afterwards, but in this study this was not the case for all young people. The research identified that more boys than girls reported having enjoyed their first sexual experience and more girls than boys clearly said they didn't like it. Research in other countries has identified a similar gender gap in the quality of experience of first sexual intercourse.[24] This is an issue that needs to be taken into account in sexuality education, particularly for girls. We understand that enjoyment often comes with experience, but this data raises some important questions. It brings us back to the discussion above regarding the gender gap in masturbation and the impact this may have on boys' and girls' sexual development and confidence. It also highlights an important task for positive relationships and sexuality education in encouraging young people to reflect on what they want and don't want and what they like and dislike in sexual interactions and how they can communicate this so that sexual interactions are enjoyable for each partner.

The importance of such discussions with young people is illustrated further when gender differences related to the enjoyment of oral and anal sex are considered. Girls give oral sex more frequently than they receive it, and when asked about enjoyment,[25] only a low percentage of the girls reported enjoying giving oral sex to a boy. In contrast, 96% of the boys rated receiving oral sex as very pleasurable and 76% said that they had enjoyed giving oral sex. Similarly, for anal sex the same kind of gender gap appears. The majority of the boys reported liking giving anal sex, which in this research was interpreted as penetrating the anus of the female partner, but only a small percentage of the girls reported enjoying it.[26]

Attempting to address why girls engage in these behaviours when they don't enjoy them was beyond the scope of the research, but in discussions with adolescent girls, we have identified that peer pressure or lack of sexual autonomy could be one of the reasons. One way of addressing this lack of equality is through comprehensive sexuality education. At home, in lessons and in one-to-one sessions with young people the above findings should inform discussions, not only to clear up any misconceptions but to emphasize the importance of young people reflecting on what they really want instead of agreeing to sexual behaviours due to pressure. Furthermore, these discussions are key in helping young people to understand what consent means. This is addressed further in Chapter 9 and later in this chapter.

Another issue to be discussed in relation to 'the first time' concerns expectations. Young people need to know that their first experience of sexual behaviour (in whatever form) may not always go smoothly and may not end in an orgasm. A movie-style experience and an orgasm shouldn't be criteria for a happy first time though. In our opinion, it's much more important that both partners felt respected and enjoyed what happened.

Finally, an important note about language. As we have said previously, a significant challenge in relationships and sexuality education concerns ambiguities around phrases and words. This is demonstrated in a recent study[27] which asked young people what they considered their 'first time' to mean. What became apparent was that young people's definitions of their 'first time' went beyond penetrative sex. Here are some examples of what young people said:

- My first time was when my partner gave me an orgasm.

- My first time was when I gave my partner an orgasm.

- My first time was when we lay naked against each other without doing anything more.

- My first time was when I had a penis in one of my body openings (and enjoyed it).

- My first time was the first time my boyfriend penetrated my vagina, and I was so happy it finally happened without pain or disappointment.

This is a great reminder of the importance of clarifying understandings when discussing relationships and sexuality with young people.

Let's get rid of the word 'virginity'

Virginity is a complex concept. To define virginity simply by saying that it means that a person has 'never had sex before' is too simple because definitions of 'sex' are problematic too. Sex is often considered to occur when a penis enters a vagina but this misses out lots of other forms of sex such as oral sex, anal sex, non-hetero sex and other non-penetrative forms of sex. Indeed, many people who have not had penis-in-vagina sex (but have had sex in other ways) don't consider themselves a virgin.

Equally, some people think virginity is only related to girls and don't consider boys as virgins or non-virgins. There are also people who consider rape or other forced sexual behaviour as not being 'real' sex, but others do. There are also young people who don't care at all about virginity, but their parents might think differently.

Traditionally, virginity was concerned with the need to protect girls against unplanned pregnancies, and in order to have physical proof of a girl's virginity, the hymen myth was developed. We call it a myth because the idea of the hymen being a thin transparent tissue that covers the entrance of the vagina is pure nonsense. The hymen is just a small ribbon of tissue around the vaginal entrance, leaving the entrance open for vaginal discharge and menstrual blood to flow out and things such as a finger, tampon, sex toy or penis to enter. The hymen varies considerably from girl to girl but might look like this:

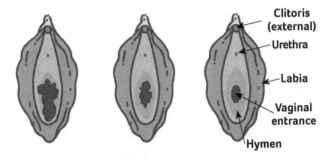

We know, however, that the vaginal opening of a so-called virgin and non-virgin are sometimes indistinguishable from each other, even for doctors! Certificates given by so-called experts to confirm that a girl is still a virgin are, therefore, worthless.

Challenging the hymen myth is an important part of relationships and sexuality education because of the pressure on girls in certain cultures to demonstrate their virginity by having an intact hymen. It is also important in relation to expectations regarding first sexual vaginal intercourse because if young people know that the hymen doesn't need to be broken, sex is more likely to be gentle and we know that around two-thirds of girls experience hardly any or no pain during their first experience of penetrative sex as long as it happens gently, with care and they are sexually aroused.[28] Equally it's important to highlight how interpretations of the term 'virginity' are complicated and also very personal. We would prefer that the term wasn't used at all because of its many negative associations, including its association with some type of loss – this may be something that you want to discuss with young people to see what their thoughts are.

Consent

Consent can be a difficult concept to explain to young people. Often it is defined as clear, verbal or non-verbal, approval from all parties, but in reality it is much more complex than this. Sometimes people may clearly say 'yes' although they don't really want to consent to sexual behaviour. For example, they may say 'yes' because they are afraid of being rejected or verbally abused by a partner if they say no or they feel they have to say yes in return for gifts such as a new mobile phone. A 'yes' can also be given by someone who doesn't have the capacity to say 'yes' because of a power difference in relation to the other person. Or a 'yes' may have been a 'yes' at the start of the act but changed into a 'no' during the act. In short, a clear 'yes' is necessary, but 'yes' doesn't always really mean 'yes'. As we discuss in Chapter 9, behaviour should also be voluntary, meaning that 'yes' only means 'yes' when it is given in a voluntary way.

Consent also plays a role in sexual behaviours when people aren't physically with one another, for example the sending of sexual pictures or videos to each other (sexting). If pictures, messages or videos are shared with third parties without consent, this is unacceptable. To make this understandable for teenagers, they need to have developed some level of empathy to be able to understand and even feel the perspective of the other person. Young people who have sent nude photos of themselves to a trusted partner who then shares them with others are often blamed for 'being so stupid to send a nude pic'. However, the person who is at fault is the person who shared the picture or video.

Sexting is an important topic to discuss as part of sexuality education, but an important point to note here is that a balanced discussion is necessary. Of course young people need to know about the possible negative consequences of sexting, but remember that it is integral to many of their relationships and can be perceived and experienced positively when consent is respected and behaviour is voluntary.[29]

Some of the complexities surrounding consent are illustrated in this real example given to us by several young female students, aged between 17 and 20 years. They all share a similar story which centres on them giving oral sex to a male partner. Before giving the boy oral sex, they all gave a voluntary 'yes', but once they had the boy's penis in their mouth, the boys would hold the girl's head down so that the penis would go deeper into her mouth and throat. The girls didn't like this but with the hands on their head they felt they couldn't escape. Some were able to discuss it afterwards with the partner, but some lacked the confidence to do so and felt upset afterwards. A similar issue emerges in 'stealthing' where men remove their condom non-consensually during penetrative sex. In both of these examples, consent is not present because the action that has been agreed to has changed, albeit in different ways.

These examples demonstrate the need to repeatedly check for consent throughout sexual interactions as well as the importance of voluntary engagement.

During relationships and sexuality education, all of these different aspects of consent should be discussed with young people. Sometimes the debates can get quite heated but they are absolutely essential, as demonstrated by the UK website Every-one's Invited (www.everyonesinvited.uk) which argues that:

> When behaviours like 'upskirting' or the non-consensual shar-ing of intimate photos are normalised this acts as a gateway to criminal acts such as sexual assault and rape. Behaviours such as misogyny, slut shaming, victim blaming, and sexual harassment create an environment where sexual violence and abuse can exist and thrive.

The Everyone's Invited website may be a useful starting point when teaching young people about consent. In Chapter 6, topic 8, we discuss how different statements and examples can be used to facilitate young people in coming up with a clear definition or description of what they consider volun-tary engagement and consent to be in different situations. Other useful tools in discussing 'consent' include the video on 'Tea Consent' (www.youtube.com/watch?v=fGoWLWS4-kU) and these materials on consent: www.bishuk.com/parents/teach-yourself-sex-ed-consent.

'Age of consent' and 'consent'

Sometimes people are confused by what is meant by 'con-sent' and the legal term 'age of consent'. Age of consent is the term used in law to outline the age a person is legally allowed to have sexual intercourse or, in some countries, the legal age at which a person is allowed to get married. The legal term 'age of consent' is used to protect children under a certain age from sexual exploitation by older people or adults. In many western countries the age of consent is usually between 16 and 18 years old; however, it would be unusual for two young people under that age who have a consensual sexual relationship to be prosecuted. So, in this latter context, the term 'consent' as we have discussed above is relevant but it is a different concept to the legal term.

Summary

In this chapter we have outlined the biopsychosocial context of adolescents' sexual behaviour and relationships. These were the key messages in this chapter:

- The ongoing development of the teenage brain has implications for their sexual development.

- A stepwise sexual career seems to be beneficial for the healthy sexual development of adolescents.

- Young people are often discovering their sexual identity and orientation at this stage, and it is important that discussions regarding sexual development encompass all identities and orientations.

- We have highlighted how vague and confusing a lot of sexual language is, for example phrases like 'the first time', 'virginity' and 'sex' mean different things to different people. So, we proposed giving young people the opportunity to define their own individual 'first time' which doesn't have to be related to penetration. We suggested getting rid of the term 'virginity' because of the many negative, unclear and stereotyping connotations.

- The complexities concerning consent were also introduced and we made some suggestions regarding how this subject could be discussed with young people.

Although research is extremely helpful in aiding our understanding, we want to conclude by emphasizing that young

people are the real experts in knowing about their own preferences and feelings. A much more detailed understanding can be
gained at the individual level by talking to young people, asking
them questions, having discussions with them and by observing them. Equally, relationships and sexuality education should
be centred on addressing what young people want and need
from us, and the best way to achieve this is to work alongside
them and let them guide the content. In the next three chapters
we will focus on specific topics in relationships and sexuality
education for different age groups that will help you meet the
needs of the young people in your lives.

Chapter 6

Early adolescence (12–14+ years)

WHAT ADULTS WANT TO KNOW

Introduction

In this and the following two chapters, we turn our attention to the 'how and what', or the practicalities, of discussing the various aspects of sexuality and relationships with adolescents. These chapters aim to answer many of the questions that parents, carers and professionals told us they needed help with when we carried out our research for this book.

As we have stressed throughout the earlier chapters, we prioritize developmental stage over age as adolescents vary so significantly developmentally. However, the existing research is age focused (as well as western focused) so we have had to refer to age for reference, but please do remember that age is only a guide when considering young people's development. We have divided the following chapters into three age categories. This chapter will discuss the needs of adolescents at 12–14+ years, Chapter 7 will be about 14–16+ years and Chapter 8 will be concerned with 16–18+ years. We realize that sometimes topics discussed in one chapter will appear in subsequent chapters, but this is necessary as the nature of the explanations need to change according to the young person's age and stage of development.

Our guidance in this and the following two chapters is based on several international guidelines and standards, namely:

- *Standards for Sexuality Education* by WHO's Regional Office for Europe and BZgA,[1] of which Sanderijn is a member of the expert group.

- UNESCO's *International Technical Guidance on Sexuality Education.*[2]

- The Sexuality Information and Education Council of the United States' *National Guidelines for Comprehensive Sexuality Education.*[3]

- Plan International's comprehensive sexuality education program standards *Putting the C in CSE: Standards for Content, Delivery and Environments of Comprehensive Sexuality Education.*[4]

- The Government of Western Australia's *Talk Soon, Talk Often.*[5]

Although the international guidelines are written for professionals, our experience is that they can also be very useful for parents, carers and sexuality education in non-professional settings. The guidelines and standards we have listed give an excellent overview of the necessary themes and topics, but they often lack advice on how to address the topics in practice; this is what we want to offer you in these chapters. We will give lots of examples and suggest certain words and approaches so that you can implement the international guidance, but remember, these are just suggestions and you are free to use whatever words work best for you and your particular context.

Most secondary schools will cover the basics of reproductive health, but what is lacking in many schools is a focus on the development of young people's opinions, values, critical thinking and autonomy. These chapters aim to support you in addressing these gaps. We are mindful that these discussions can be sensitive and that adolescents might have strong opinions that may differ from yours, so we not only give examples of how to communicate accurate and factual knowledge, but we also provide examples of how you might go about discussing the more sensitive issues and explore the young person's own opinions.

Chapters 7 and 8 have a similar structure. Using the guidelines above, alongside our research for this book, we have selected several topics that young people want or need to know about. We have used questions from carers, parents, teachers and other professionals to shape these discussions, and in our responses we aim to provide you with suggestions for how you may wish to discuss these issues with a young person or a group of young people. These suggestions are not intended to be prescriptive; instead we hope that you use them to develop your own ideas as to how you could have similar conversations with young people.

What's it like to be 12–14?

Depending upon your particular education system, during this stage many young people will make the transition to a larger school with older year groups. With this change, they will be making a huge transition from being one of the oldest in school to being one of the youngest. They need to adjust to new peers, build new friendships and adapt to new rules and values as well as an unfamiliar building, new teachers, new subjects, more books, more homework and, often, a different journey to school. With this transition, children tend to mature and transform rapidly into young adults, with parents struggling to keep up with the seemingly overnight change from baby to adolescent!

Alongside all of these social changes, most young people of this age experience significant physical changes due to the production of hormones as we have discussed in Chapter 4. The prefrontal cortex in the brain is not yet fully developed, meaning that emotions are dominant, which is why this stage of development is often characterized by mood-swings and a need to immediately satisfy impulses and desires. For example, seeing a friend with the latest mobile phone might trigger a strong desire for them to have one too, and immediately! Young people of this age tend to act first and think afterwards, which can lead to impulsive decision making and behaviours. There is often a strong desire to be more independent and 12–14 year olds often become more aware of who they are and how others might perceive them. Their self-identity is developing in a more conscious way, meaning that the question of 'Who am I?' becomes increasingly important. At the same time, the production of sex hormones can make them feel strange, awkward or lonely. They can feel overwhelmed by these sexual feelings, not yet knowing what to do with them, or they may begin to experiment by exploring their own body and masturbate. In addition, their not-yet-developed prefrontal cortex can make it difficult for them to problem solve.

Topic 1: Talking about puberty

Question from a biology teacher:

'I need to teach a class of 12–13 year olds about puberty, as part of their relationships and sexuality education. This is the first time I have taught this and I am guessing that most of my students will know most of the biology already. How can I make my lessons more interesting for them?'

Question from a parent:

'I think my child knows about puberty but I feel I need to make sure. How should I do this?'

It's a misconception to assume that adolescents already know about sexuality issues, including how their bodies work. They may talk a lot about sexuality or appear knowledgeable and many will be going through or have gone through puberty, but we know that there are many misunderstandings and gaps in knowledge among this age group.[6]

As a teacher, you may want to do a short anonymized survey with your students in which you tell them that your next lesson will be on puberty and you ask them what they really want to know. You will probably be surprised to see what they still want to know! You can then structure the lesson around their needs. Depending upon the dynamics of the group, you might also find it useful to develop a quiz for them to answer in small groups. Better still, you could ask the students to write several general (not personal) questions for their peers to respond to. With all of these approaches, you could finish your lesson with a short debate in groups to encourage your students to build their own ideas and opinions.

By this stage it's important that young people understand how bodies develop and change both on the inside and the outside during puberty and that the speed of these changes varies from person to person. They need to know that the physical changes are concerned with preparing their bodies to reproduce and are brought about by the production of sex hormones. These sex hormones can also cause sexual feelings which can sometimes be confusing or overwhelming, but this is normal and will be happening to some of their friends too. They should also know that their mood may go up and down during puberty and that there are adults around them who love them and are willing to support them. We deal with additional information about puberty below.

At home, carers and parents can ask their children what relationships and sexuality education they have covered at school as a way into addressing any gaps in knowledge and discussing values. Below, we have outlined an example of part of a conversation between a father and his 12 year old son that you may find useful:

Father: *'What have you learnt about in Relationships and Sexuality Education at school so far?'*

Son: *'Oh just something about how bodies change during puberty and why girls have periods and that sort of stuff. But I already knew about all that.'*

Father: *'What's the funniest thing you've learned about puberty?'*

Son: *'Uhm... that some boys grow small boobs! I hope it doesn't happen to me!'*

Father: *'If it happens, you know it will only be temporary, don't you? It's just because of the hormonal ups and downs that happen at this stage. What do you think you'll do if you do grow little breasts?'*

Son: *'I'll be so embarrassed... I'll go mad!'*

Father: *'If it happens, you'll be prepared so it won't be so bad, but don't worry about it too much. I'll be there to listen to you and support you. We will work it out together. Tell me though, what parts of puberty are you looking forward to?'*

Son: *'Feeling grown up, being allowed to do more on my own and getting more respect from other kids. That'll be good.'*

Topic 2: The vulva

Question from a biology teacher:

'I'm finding that my textbooks give quite limited information about the female genital tract with just one sentence about the clitoris and nothing about the hymen. Help!'

Question from a parent:

> *'My son of 12 wants to know what the female genitals look like.*
> *I've just realized that I probably only told him about his body*
> *and genitals. So what can I tell him?'*

It's important for young people to understand their bodies and we agree that although most biology books address the male genital tract quite comprehensively, the female genital tract is rarely explained in detail. The same often applies to parental explanations. So, here's a description of what we think young people at this stage will find helpful. See also the following illustration which shows the external part of the clitoris at the top of the vulva and the anus and buttocks at the bottom of the illustration. The numbers on the illustration correspond with the numbers used in the descriptions below.

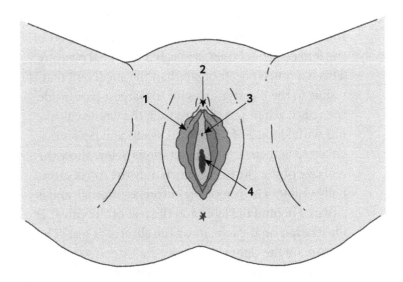

The illustration above shows the outer and inner labia (1), the external part of the clitoris at the top (2), below is the urethra (the tiny hole) (3), then the vagina (the larger hole) (4). These are described below.

The female genitals are called the vulva and consist of:

1. **Vulva-lips or labia.** These are the lips surrounding the vaginal opening and urethra (pee-hole). There are two outer labia and two inner labia. Before puberty the outer labia neatly cover the inner labia which are usually a bit smaller. But during puberty the inner labia grow and can become larger than the outer labia and they may become uneven in size. The colour of the vulva and labia often changes too and the area becomes more moist. Adolescents need to know that these changes are absolutely normal. The moistness of the vulva shouldn't be a cause for concern and 'intimate sprays' or other 'intimate body care' products are not necessary and may cause irritation.

2. **Clitoris.** At the top of the vulva (i.e. the point that is furthest away from the anus) where the labia meet, the clitoris is found. This is the most sensitive part of the female genital tract, dedicated to sexual pleasure. This is a much bigger organ than the small bud that is visible in the illustration, with the largest part inside the vulva. When sexually aroused, the whole vulva fills with blood and the clitoris swells and becomes enlarged and erect. The illustrations below show the real size of the clitoris of which only the top is externally visible. The rest of the clitoris is internal, and is situated behind the labia and the rest of the vulva. The illustration on the left shows the clitoris 'at rest'. The picture on the right shows how the clitoris swells due to increased blood flow during sexual arousal.

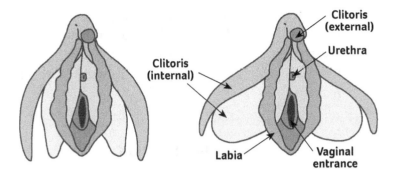

3. **Urethra.** This is the opening in the vulva where urine comes out. It's usually a small opening in between the vaginal opening and the top of the clitoris. The area around the urethra can become sensitive during sexual arousal, as well as the rest of the vulva.

4. **Vagina and hymen.** The opening to the vagina is at the lower part of the vulva. The vagina is a tube, but when not sexually aroused the tube walls and the opening are more or less closed. The vagina can be around 10 cm long and ends at the cervix, the entrance to the uterus. Although there are other ways of getting pregnant, the vagina is an important part of reproduction because it allows the penis to enter, and if the man ejaculates, the semen can travel through the cervix to the uterus where fertilization may take place. It is also the means by which the majority of babies are born and it allows menstrual blood to flow from the uterus. The walls of the vagina have hardly any nerves. Just inside the opening of the vagina is the hymen, about which there are many myths, as we highlighted in Chapter 5. The hymen is *not* a thin tissue covering the opening of the vagina. It is just a 'ribbon' of tissue positioned along the vaginal opening. A hymen, therefore, does not have to be broken or bleed when something (a finger, sex toy, tampon or penis) enters the vagina for the first

time. In some countries 'hymen repair' or 'virginity repair' surgery has become fashionable, although this is extremely controversial with calls for it to be banned internationally. See also Chapter 5 for some pictures of hymens.

Topic 3: Menstruation

Question from a single dad:

'I'm sure my 12 year old daughter knows what menstruation is but what kind of practical things does she need to know before her periods start? I'm also wondering what my son, age 13, should know about menstruation?'

Question from a teacher:

'I teach young people about reproduction and I will be teaching menstruation next week. I am fine with the technical aspects of menstruation but what practical issues are girls and boys likely to want to hear about?'

Although learning about the menstrual cycle in biology is important, children and adolescents have needs that extend beyond biological knowledge. In advance of the lesson about menstruation, a teacher could ask the students to write down three questions about menstruation anonymously and these could shape the content of the lesson. Similarly, a parent could ask their child (of whatever gender) what questions they have about menstruation and this could serve as the basis for future conversations. However, it's important to recognize that some young people might not know what they don't know and you may need to fill in gaps that their questions don't cover.

In our experience young people want to know things like:

- How much blood does a girl lose during her period?

- Is it painful?

- Do girls feel ill during their period?

- Do girls need to stay off school when they're having a period?

- Will the hymen break if they use a tampon?

- What sanitary products are best?

- Can they go swimming and do sport during their periods?

- Can you get pregnant when menstruating?

Here's some guidance that you may find useful in answering these questions:

- Typical blood loss during a period is one soup spoon of blood daily with less than this towards the end of the period. It might look like more than this, but it rarely is. 'Older' blood looks brownish and 'fresh' blood looks red.

- Losing the blood doesn't hurt, but most girls have a cramping pain in the lower abdomen or back and/or breast tenderness just before and during their periods. Some also feel nauseous, have headaches and/or feel dizzy. Heat pads and painkillers can ease the discomfort. If regular painkillers don't alleviate the pain, alternatives should be prescribed.

- Some feel uncomfortable but not ill. Others sometimes need a day off from school.

- Tampon usage doesn't break the hymen since the hymen doesn't cover the vaginal opening (see also above in topic 2 and in Chapter 5). Younger girls may find it helpful to use smaller tampons and they may find that they get on better with applicator tampons, although others prefer non-applicator tampons. Equally though, some girls don't like using tampons and get on perfectly well with sanitary towels. Supermarkets and pharmacies sell a huge variety of sanitary towels, as well as tampons, and it's a good idea to try out the different brands and sizes.

- Teachers are strongly advised to have sanitary towels available for girls, as some girls may be unprepared for their first (or subsequent) periods and some may not be able to afford sanitary products. Making sanitary products available in schools may encourage girls who experience 'period poverty' to attend school rather than miss it each month because of the stress associated with not having access to sanitary towels and tampons.

- Girls can carry on and do sport or go swimming during their periods and some find that this helps with period pain. However, if the first few days are quite uncomfortable it may be better to just take things a little easier than usual. For swimming it is advised to use tampons and many girls find tampons better for sports such as gymnastics and dance, but be aware that some girls may be unfamiliar with tampons.

- It is possible to become pregnant during menstruation. Although a 12 year old may not think pregnancy is relevant to them, we know from experience that it's a good idea to discuss this topic at a young age because there are many misconceptions around it. If the individual has short or irregular cycles, ovulation may occur during the last few days of the period meaning that it is possible for reproduction to occur. Menstruation must not, therefore, be used as a form of contraception.

Finally, it's important to involve boys in all your lessons or discussions about menstruation. By doing this it doesn't become just a 'girl's thing', but something that is also relevant to their lives. Menstruation should be seen as a normal part of life and should not be something that is embarrassing or dirty. Making tampons and pads openly available in every bathroom at home or school can help to remove any shame or embarrassment associated with menstruation.

Topic 4: Body image

Question from a parent about their 12 year old daughter and 14 year old son:

'My children are obsessed with the "insta-look" and I'm worried that it's getting out of control. Am I right to be concerned?'

We hear many parents and carers voice these concerns, but this is also an issue of concern for many teachers and other professionals. Worries may centre on young people dieting, over exercising, taking muscle-building supplements, wearing sexualized clothes and lingerie, spending hours on hair and make-up before leaving home, posing rather than enjoying the moment... the list goes on!

As adults, it's important to understand that adolescents largely have one thing in common: they want to be liked. As we saw in Chapter 4, identity development is an important stage of development around now and it can make many young people feel insecure. Concerns about how peers perceive them frequently becomes central to young people's thinking, and high levels of insecurity and/or low self-confidence can result in them wanting to look a certain way in order to belong to certain groups. This need for 'belonging' can make young people feel safe but it can also make some adolescents vulnerable to peer pressure, and they may adopt behaviours because they are afraid of being rejected.

Although adults tell young people to be authentic and to be themselves, the fear of losing their peers' approval and becoming isolated can be so strong that this is an unrealistic expectation. Knowing this can help parents and carers understand why some adolescents choose to engage in extreme behaviours. Trying to change their bodies is one such behaviour, for example dieting and using high doses of supplements to build muscles are not uncommon at this age. According to research with young people in Europe and Canada,[7] around 36% of 15 year old girls considered themselves overweight and had a negative body image, although just 14% were actually overweight. Dieting during adolescence doesn't necessarily mean that a young person has an eating disorder, as long as the diet is nutritionally healthy and is a temporary measure. However, if it becomes unhealthy or extreme, it is essential that the young person receives professional support. Similarly, extreme exercise and body building can be associated with physical and mental health risks and require professional intervention.

Sexualized clothes and lingerie, make-up and highly styled or extreme haircuts are another aspect of developing an identity and belonging to a group. For some young people, the kind of clothes and underwear they wear or how they style their hair can become a matter of being accepted or rejected. Developing an adult 'look' is also a symbolic final break with infancy and may coincide with young people throwing away their childhood toys and wanting to transform their bedrooms and/or asserting themselves verbally with their parents. They want to show the world that they want to be treated as an adult, not a child.

So, to answer the question 'Am I right to be concerned?', these behaviours are all completely understandable, but they do pose some risks. For example, extreme dieting, eating disorders, over exercising and excessive body building can all present significant risks to young people physically and need to be recognized as such and acted upon. With regards to choice of clothing, underwear, make-up and hairstyles, parents and carers may feel uncomfortable at seeing their child(ren) transform into young adults and this can result in conflict, but our position is that this, for some young people, is an important aspect of self-expression. However, if a 12 year old looks eight years older than they really are, this can pose a risk in terms of their personal safety because they will be approached by the outside world as more mature than they actually are. Although some teenagers would welcome such an approach, it can become problematic when the other person has sexual expectations.

Topic 5: Porn

Porn is often of great concern to carers, parents and teachers alike. This is a question from a teacher regarding 12–13 year old boys:

'Some boys watch porn on their mobiles during their lunch breaks. One of the girls told me because a porn clip was sent to her by accident. How should I deal with this?'

Watching porn on devices is quite common at this age[8] and sharing porn with classmates gives some boys status at school. Schools usually have a policy that watching porn in and around school is strictly prohibited. As a teacher, you can invoke this policy through your usual disciplinary procedures but you can go beyond this by raising the young people's awareness of the ethics of the porn industry. You could tell them about the different kinds of porn, ethical versus exploitative, violent versus female-friendly porn etc. Critical media skills and critical reflection on what they see or search for can be more informative than just telling them that porn is bad and watching porn is prohibited because of the school policy. Parents can have the same discussions with their children.

We know that rules and explanations won't guarantee that adolescents will never watch porn again. However, clear discussions about porn and what you consider to be kind and healthy sexual behaviours and relationships will give clear messages about your position on porn and values about sexual relationships. For helpful tools and suggestions about how to discuss porn with teenagers, see also www.bishuk.com.

Topic 6: Safer sex and sexually transmitted infections (STIs)

Question from a parent:

> 'What should I tell my teenagers about STIs? I assume school will tell them a lot about the risks?'

While we promote a positive approach to sexuality education and we are concerned that too often the focus of relationships and sexuality education is on warnings and risks while forgetting to mention that sexual behaviour can be pleasurable, parents and carers are right in wanting their children to know about STIs. Schools (should) give at least the minimal factual information about STIs and most adolescents know the basics, but you may be surprised as to how many misconceptions exist among adolescents with regard to STIs. According to a Dutch study[9] with young people aged 12–25 years, about 40% believed that you can wash away an STI after having had unprotected sexual intercourse and about the same percentage didn't know that girls can become infertile as a result of some STIs. This is despite most of these young people having received regular relationships and sexuality education at school.

Regular conversations at home about these issues are, therefore, very important. In Chapter 3 we gave some suggestions about how to start these kinds of conversations which you may find useful in this context, but checking what your child already knows and believes and identifying what the gaps are could be the first step. Here is a brief overview of some facts about STIs:[10]

- STIs are infections that are passed from one person to another through sexual contact. These include chlamydia, gonorrhoea, genital herpes, genital warts, human papillomavirus (HPV), syphilis and HIV. Many of these STIs don't show symptoms for a long time. Even without symptoms, they can still be harmful and passed on during sex.

- Anyone who is sexually active can get an STI. You don't even have to 'go all the way' (have anal or vaginal sex) to get an STI. This is because some STIs, like herpes, genital warts and HPV, are spread by skin-to-skin contact.

- The best way to protect against any STI is to use a condom during sexual penetration. To protect against HPV, girls and boys can be vaccinated before they have their first penetrative sexual encounter.

- Safer ways of having sex could be mutual masturbation, kissing, hugging and discovering each other's body and genitals.

For further information see:

- www.cdc.gov

- www.plannedparenthood.org

- www.advocatesforyouth.org

- www.brook.org.uk

- www.bishuk.com.

When discussing STIs, helping teenagers to build their values around these topics is also important. For example, you may want to discuss with them how they would perceive someone who got infected by an STI and how they would feel if this happened to their best friend. Stigmatization of people with STIs can be incredibly damaging to the individual[11] and can be prevented by giving accurate information about modes of transmission and by having discussions with young people about stigma in a way that is meaningful to them. Films, documentaries and dramas, for example *It's a Sin*, can be a useful trigger for such discussions.

In relation to safe sex, this has traditionally been concerned with preventing STI transmission as reflected in the discussions above. But the prevention of an unplanned pregnancy and emotional safety are equally important aspects of safe sex. Coercion and pressure make sex unsafe for the individual and this needs to be an integral part of any conversation about safety.

When discussing safe sex with your teenagers, you could ask them to think through how to make sexual behaviour safe and enjoyable at the same time. This kind of question is likely to be more helpful than a risk-orientated one-way conversation as it will be more meaningful and positive. Sexual behaviour shouldn't be based on fear but on enjoyment, and avoiding risks while having pleasure can happily go together.

Topic 7: Contraception

Question from a parent and a teacher:

> *'What should young people know about contraception at this stage?'*

Although many young people won't be intending to engage in sexual behaviour at this stage, the use of contraception, including emergency contraception (also known as the 'morning after pill'), should become a normal aspect of sexual health discussions. At this stage, young people are capable of learning about all the different methods of contraception.

We have chosen not to go into detail regarding specific contraceptives as they change so rapidly and availability varies internationally, but instead we recommend that you refer to the following websites which hold the most recent information:

- www.plannedparenthood.org

- www.brook.org.uk

- www.your-life.com/en

- www.advocatesforyouth.org

- www.bishuk.com.

'Advocates for Youth', a US organization promoting relationships and sexuality education for teens, also has some great resources for teaching young people about contraception. You can find a lesson plan here: www.advocatesforyouth.org/wp-content/uploads/storage/advfy/lesson-plans/lesson-plan-contraception-part-i-and-ii.pdf

When doing a lesson like this, bringing examples of the different types of contraception to the classroom would be a good idea. If a school doesn't allow teachers to show real contraceptives, pictures and leaflets with detailed information work well too.

Just a note about male condoms as they are used so widely internationally. The first point to make is that condoms really do take some practice to use correctly, so although it can create a lot of excitement we do advise teachers and parents to show young people how to use them and let them practise on models. Key points are addressed in the six steps of correct condom usage below:

1. Check the date.

2. Open the package carefully *not* using scissors, sharp nails or teeth.

3. Check which way the condom unrolls – unrolling a condom inside out is difficult but lots of inexperienced people still do it!

4. Place the condom on the tip of the erect penis or model and squeeze the top of it.

5. Keeping the top of the condom squeezed, unroll the condom to the bottom of the erect penis or model.

6. After use, roll it off and throw it away.

It is also important that young people are aware that there are many different types and brands of condoms, and if they don't get on with the first one they try, they can try out different brands. However, it is essential that the condoms they choose meet international standards.

Topic 8: Consent

Here is a question from a teacher; we have had similar questions from parents too:

'Is "consent" relevant to younger adolescents such as those aged 12–13?'

The answer is yes, consent is highly relevant to this age group and for younger children too. Consent is about much more than saying no to sexual harassment. As we have explained in Chapter 5, consent is about being clear that both parties agree to a sexual act, but consent is a complex concept because clarity of communication isn't always easy and saying 'yes' or 'no' isn't always easy either, depending upon the relationship and the context. Sometimes a 'yes' isn't a true 'yes' because of coercion or pressure and a 'yes' can become a 'no' during the act. Consent is also related to empathy and the ability to be able to imagine other people's emotions which some young people at this stage may have not yet fully developed.

Discussing the importance of consent with young people as well as the possible consequences of continuing a sexual act without consent could be the first and an important part of a discussion regarding consent.[12] Next, a discussion regarding the definition of consent could be facilitated through small-group discussions using mind maps. Following this, groups could explore scenarios in which consent was or wasn't clearly given and what could have been done differently to ensure that consent was upheld. You could conclude with a plenary discussion using provocative questions or statements like:

- Is a verbal 'yes' always a 'yes'?

- What role does 'seduction' play in relation to 'consent'?

- Can a drunk person give consent?

- How can someone with more power make a situation more 'consensual'?

These and other statements, as well as some great examples of lessons and methods to teach consent to young people, can be found on this website: www.bishuk.com.

Topic 9: Sexual identity

Question from a parent:

'We always thought that my son Dan, who is now 13, would be gay. He has always been very gentle and sensitive, preferring stereotypical girls' toys and games. We've had no problem with this but when we have raised the issue of sexual identity with him, he's always found it a very difficult conversation. Although most of his friends are girls, he has recently become friends with two boys who he goes to football matches with, although up

until now he has hated football. He also wants to start body building and he recently told us that he has a girlfriend. We're confused. Does this mean that he's straight?'

Most young people discover their sexual identity during adolescence or just before puberty starts. According to research in the Netherlands,[13] many adolescents are happy with their sexual identity regardless of what it is, but this is definitely not the case for every young person. Some find being attracted to the same sex confusing and anxiety provoking. What we also see in the Dutch research[14] is that during adolescence, young people make a distinction between being attracted to the same sex, self-appointment (calling yourself gay/lesbian/bi) and sexual behaviour with the same sex. This means that although someone may feel attracted to the same sex, they may not label themselves gay/lesbian/bi. The same applies to sexual experiences with people of the same sex; young people might have sexual experiences with someone of the same sex without calling themselves homosexual. Between 12 and 15 years of age, many young people are still working out their sexual identity and it is only as they grow older that this becomes clearer. Falling in love with someone of the same sex at age 13 doesn't, therefore, automatically mean that the individual is homosexual or bisexual, and likewise, falling in love with someone of the opposite sex at this age doesn't necessarily mean that the individual is heterosexual (see Chapter 5).

Adolescence is a time for young people to discover themselves, who they are, what they want and what they value. To discover all of this, they need to have the opportunity to have several experiences and to make mistakes. Self-discovery doesn't occur in a vacuum or as a separate entity to other aspects of a young person's life. In relation to Dan, this question suggests that he's in the midst of discovering his sexual identity. His own previous preferences regarding friends and play may have confused him as he grew older and became more aware of heteronormative messages. Like many young adolescents, he may have also felt intimidated by his peers and felt pressured to conform to mainstream behaviours in order to avoid becoming vulnerable to bullying. Young people who are struggling with their sexual or gender identity can feel very insecure and vulnerable and to be verbally, and potentially physically, abused is their greatest fear. Adjusting to what is expected by the majority can be one coping strategy. It's also quite common for some adolescents who are unsure about their sexual identity to experiment with different types of sexual relationships and to hide any clues that may betray their inner desires and dreams because they find their wider environment fearful and intimidating. In this case, giving Dan the opportunity to find his way and discover who he is, by supporting his choices, not being judgemental and letting him know that you are there for him whenever he needs you, will allow him to discover his sexual identity in his own time.

Topic 10: The impact of media on views regarding relationships, gender and sexuality

Question from a parent:

'My two teens (13 and 14) are crazy about TV programmes like "Temptation Island", "Love Island" and "Big Brother". Will watching these kinds of programmes influence their ideas about sex and relationships?'

Many things can have an influence on a young person's ideas about sex and relationships. For some these types of TV shows can, among other things, influence ideas about sexuality and relationships, but discussions with you can too. Even if you hate these types of programmes, if you watch them with your teenagers this can provide a great opportunity to discuss, debate and share your opinions and values with them. At this stage of development you still play an important role in contributing to the development of your children's personal values. Sharing in this way will also help you in staying connected with your child (see also Chapter 1). Asking questions like 'who is your favourite?', 'who do you think will win?' and 'do you think other people like to look like that?' are 'showing-interest' questions and not 'controlling' questions. These are questions to start a discussion with your teenagers and invite them to share some personal thoughts with you about their perspectives on sexuality and relationships. By asking questions you can also check their understandings and drop in some factual information to correct any misinterpretations. Try to approach the experience with curiosity. Showing an interest in your teenagers' opinions in an equal way will mean a lot to them and enable you to help them to develop their critical thinking.

Topic 11: Masturbation

Question from a parent:

'What should I tell my young teenagers about masturbation?'

Many parents find masturbation one of the most difficult topics to discuss with teenagers. They say that it feels uncomfortable to talk about a topic that is so intimate and personal. Our opinion is that talking about masturbation is not an absolute must if it feels too awkward, but you may wish to convey certain messages such as: it's OK, it is a personal choice, both boys/men, girls/women and non-binary people can do it, it's a private activity and a great opportunity to learn about your own body as well as what you like and dislike. And if one decides not to do it, it's OK too. (In Chapter 7, topic 4, we discuss more about female masturbation.) The younger the child, the easier it is to convey these messages, but even if you haven't discussed masturbation prior to this stage it is still possible. For example, you may wish to give your teenager a book on sexuality education in

which these positive messages are expressed or perhaps by raising these points as part of a more general discussion. However,
for many parents, a direct conversation is completely doable.
Here's an example that you may find helpful:

Parent to 12 year old son while changing son's bed together:
*'Do you remember me talking to you about your first ejacu-
lation? It will probably happen quite soon.'*

Son: *'Yeah, I know. When will it happen?'*

Parent: *'Do you remember me saying how it might happen
when you are asleep if you have an exciting dream about
something sexy. Or it can happen when you touch your penis
and it becomes stiff – do you know what I'm talking about,
it's called masturbation?'*

Son: *'I'm not sure.'*

Parent: *'Masturbation is when you touch your penis in such
a way that it feels good and becomes erect and it can lead
to a really special feeling which is called an orgasm. Once
you've reached puberty, the orgasm will be accompanied by
an ejaculation. It means your body has made sperm for the
first time, which is a sign that you're really growing up! You
probably already know, but this also means that your body is
capable of making a baby if you were to have sex with a girl.'*

Son: *'Yeah, I know that already. I had lessons in school about
reproduction and babies. But I don't really understand masturbation. Do you mean "jerking off"? How do I do that to
get an orgasm?'*

Parent: *'There are many ways. Some people like to use one hand
and gently push and pull the skin of the penis up and down,
others combine it with rubbing the penis on something else.
You'll find out for yourself in your own way.'*

Son: *'Can girls masturbate?'*

Parent: *'Yes they can – adult women too. Most people can but not everyone wants to – it's everybody's personal choice. But if you do, be gentle and care for yourself; in fact some people prefer to call masturbation "solo-sex" or "self-care behaviour". I think that's a nice way to express it.'*

Please see Chapter 7, topic 4, for a discussion regarding masturbation and orgasm in girls.

Chapter 7

Mid-adolescence (14–16+ years)

WHAT ADULTS WANT TO KNOW

What's it like to be 14–16?

Most 14 to 16 year olds no longer consider themselves children. Most girls will have started their periods and most boys will have ejaculated. They are, therefore, physically capable of becoming parents. Brain development, in interaction with social factors, is still ongoing and young people of this age are often looking for thrills and immediate rewards. Because of this, they may begin to experiment with alcohol, smoking, drugs and sexual behaviours. This can be a confusing period for adolescents, with many longing for independence but, at the same time, needing boundaries. Relationships with parents and carers can often become challenging and conflicting because of this. By this stage, most young people will have good verbal skills and may enjoy engaging in strong debates with adults and expressing their opinions, emotions and thoughts. Many will have experienced romantic feelings by now and they will often begin to develop romantic relationships at this stage. A minority may have previously engaged in sexual intercourse but intimate behaviours such as touching each other's genitals over and under clothes is more common and, increasingly, young people's first sexual interactions may be online, for example by sharing nude or half nude pictures, by masturbating together online or sharing sexual text messages.

Below we have addressed key topics that arose from our research for this book, while taking account of the international guidelines outlined in Chapter 6. Throughout, we acknowledge that this can be a particularly exciting time for young people, and our suggestions aim to support you in helping young people develop skills in critical thinking so that they can make well-informed decisions that are right for them.

Topic 1: Starting sexual relationships

Question from a group of parents of 15 year olds at a relationships and sexuality education session:

'Our children are reaching an age where some friendships are developing into more romantic ones. It seems quite likely that at least one of them will start a sexual relationship soon. We want them to be confident and prepared and to be safe too. We have already discussed the basics of STIs and protection and they've got access to condoms. Is there anything more we should do?'

Well done on having already done the groundwork as well as thinking ahead! In addition to the messages that we covered in the previous chapter, at this stage young people need more detailed information about how to make sexual behaviour pleasurable and safe. You might want to chat to them about first time sex with a partner not always being easy. It can be messy and confusing, but it can also be a lot of fun. It doesn't have to end in an orgasm as there are a lot of things that can be done together which are enjoyable without having an orgasm. You could also chat to them about being creative and curious and checking regularly on whether their partner is still OK. Remind them that they should stop if anything hurts.

Going back to our first point, you could suggest that they don't focus too much on being 'successful'. Sex together is not a technical procedure between two bodies, it's all about being intimate. Being intimate is about much more than achieving an orgasm or experiencing penetration. Being intimate means being emotionally bonded. Your adolescents may have already fantasized about their first sexual experience, but the reality might be quite different. It may be less than expected or maybe much better, but either way it will be a learning process.

Because you have been open with your teenagers previously this may be a comfortable conversation, but be aware that even the most open adolescents can find more specific conversations like this a bit awkward. If this is the case, you might want to check what information they have already received from school and you could use some of the websites we listed in Chapter 6 (topic 6) to help you convey the following key messages for this age group:

- A priority for making the first experience enjoyable is to make it safe. When you feel safe, there is more room to enjoy the experience and be curious and creative.

- Some specific sexual behaviours are more risky in relation to STIs/HIV and unplanned pregnancy than others. A good source to support you in having this conversation is www.brook.org.uk.

- Anal sex (penis in anus) is uncommon at this age but your children should know that because the anus has no natural lubrication, it's important to use a water-based lubricant, to use a condom that is designed for anal sex, to be gentle when penetrating and to agree beforehand how to signal if it hurts and that you wish to stop.

- Oral sex is completely safe in relation to pregnancy but might be unsafe in relation to STIs/HIV.

- When the sexual history of a partner is unknown or if the person has an STI, a condom or 'dental dam' is advised for oral sex. A 'dental dam' is a soft latex or polyurethane square, which is used to cover the anus, or female genital area, during oral sex. It can be easily made from cutting a condom into a square, if not available.

- STIs can be transmitted during same-sex behaviours and not only through penetrative sexual behaviours. Good websites are: www.yoursexualhealthmatters. org.uk/further-sexual-health-support/lgbt and www.teenplaybook.org/what-if/lgbtq-guide.

We advise against showing pictures of STIs such as warts and herpes on people's genitals in both the school and home context as fear-based messages such as these are ineffective. Teenagers tend to shut their eyes (and ears) when anxiety-provoking images like these are shown, meaning that they stop listening. They could even become anxious about being touched intimately as part of a romantic relationship. This isn't the aim of effective sexuality education.

Topic 2: Access to contraception

Question from the same group of parents in the previous question:

> 'What about contraceptives for our teens? As they are all around 15, access to contraceptives might be problematic.'

Condoms are generally the easiest contraception for young people to obtain, as they are widely available in shops and pharmacies, although many young people find the embarrassment of purchasing them off-putting. So it's great that you've made condoms available already, but do remind your teenagers about how to use condoms safely (see Chapter 6, topic 7). To obtain other forms of contraception, access to a health care professional is required and, depending upon the country/state/region, sometimes girls under 18 can't be prescribed contraception or, sometimes, parental consent is required. If this is the case in your region, we would encourage you to advocate for your daughter. Access to emergency contraception (the 'morning after pill') also varies across countries, states and regions but should be promoted for use if a condom isn't used or if it becomes damaged or slips off, preferably within 48 hours. If you know in advance where your child can obtain emergency contraception, much stress and panic can be avoided.

A note for teachers

Discussing the variety of contraception available for teenagers at this age is absolutely essential. Many biology textbooks discuss the basics of contraception, but as a teacher you can do more. You could show your students the different methods and devices and let them feel them and discuss them. In countries where the availability of contraception for teenagers is problematic, you could contact a local youth-friendly health centre and invite one of the health care workers to school. You could also invite a family doctor/nurse or hospital doctor/nurse to come and bring contraception to show the students and explain to them what they can do when they need contraception, for example which organizations or doctors are youth friendly, whether their parents will need to give their consent and how confidentiality is maintained.

Topic 3: Discussing sexual orientation in a resistant context

Question from a teacher for 15–16 year olds:

> 'Our school is in a traditional area and many families here have a negative attitude towards homosexuality. I try to be open and positive in my lessons when discussing sexual diversity, but there's a lot of resistance from some of the students. I'm aware that this is making a couple of students in the class unhappy as they identify as LGBTIQ+. Do you have any suggestions for how I can change the atmosphere in my class to make it more supportive of sexual diversity?'

Sexual diversity is integral to comprehensive sexuality education. All of the international guidelines include sexual diversity in their list of topics that should be addressed, even for countries where the topic is considered sensitive. However, through our work with teachers we know how challenging discussing these topics in the classroom setting can be. We suggest that discussions should be based on facts and that the differences between facts and opinions are explored, emphasizing that opinions are often based on emotions, religious beliefs or cultural norms rather than facts. Personal opinions can be given of course, not as facts but as clear opinions, and should be addressed as such as well. You could ask your students to work in groups to find at least five correct facts about sexual diversity, using reliable data, and ask them to present their findings to the class. Facts may include:

- definitions, e.g. of LGBTIQ+, sexual diversity or homosexuality

- statistics, e.g. how many LGBTIQ+ people live in their country

- the challenges people who identify as LGBTIQ+ commonly experience

- the law, e.g. what the law says about homosexuality

- cultural aspects, e.g. what different cultures or religions say about the topic and establishing whether these are facts or opinions.

Once the students have collected and checked all these facts about sexual diversity, they could finally make a list of personal values or opinions. This may be best done anonymously. In this way sexual diversity can be discussed with respect to personal and religious beliefs. It's also important to discuss the impact of stigmatizing behaviours, including 'banter' about sexual diversity, on non-hetero young people. We know that mental health issues like depression, anxiety and suicide are more frequent among young people who identify as LGBTIQ+, especially when growing up in societies, environments or families where sexual diversity is not accepted (see also www.stonewall.org.uk). Young people who are LGBTIQ+ need to feel safe, accepted and supported. Showing supportive and challenging film footage can be a powerful way to start debates. You may find the movie *Call Me By My Name*, YouTube movies about the impact of homophobic bullying like www.youtube.com/watch?v=fFJrgl7qp7M, *It Gets Better* by Todrick Hall or different versions of the YouTube anti-bullying movie with Coldplay's 'Fix You' useful. Although all of these interventions will contribute to the development of a safe atmosphere in your class, remember just one lesson isn't enough to change deep-rooted homophobic beliefs and values.

Topic 4: Female masturbation and orgasm

Question from a parent:

'My daughter wants to know whether it's normal for girls to masturbate and she has asked me to tell her how she can experience an orgasm. What should I say?'

It's great that your daughter feels comfortable enough to ask you these questions. You can reassure her that masturbation is absolutely normal for girls at this age. In terms of explaining how to experience an orgasm, your daughter needs to understand the anatomy of the vulva. As we explained in Chapter 6, the vulva is an organ consisting of different parts: the vulva lips (inner and outer lips or labia), the vagina and the vaginal opening, the hymen, the urethra and the clitoris. Girls also need to know that their clitoris is a large organ mostly hidden inside the body on the inner side of the vulva, with only a small bud visible at the top of the vulva. The clitoris is a highly sensitive organ that can become erect and stiff when touched or when a girl is sexually aroused. It is only by stimulating the clitoris that girls can experience an orgasm. Stimulating the vagina, by penetration of a penis, dildo or finger, doesn't usually lead to an orgasm because the vaginal walls are insensitive and the clitoris isn't stimulated. One small spot just inside the vagina, the G-spot, can be thinner than the rest of the vaginal lining and some women can reach an orgasm by stimulating the area because the inner part of the clitoris is situated just behind it. However, this only happens among a small proportion of sexually experienced women and can be quite difficult to achieve.

You can explain to your daughter that exploring her body and finding the outside bud of the clitoris and gently rubbing it is a very personal experience and is the best way to reach an orgasm. When feeling sexually aroused, the other parts of the vulva like the inner lips, the skin around the entrance of the vagina, as well as between the urethra and vaginal opening, can also become highly sensitive because the inner part of the clitoris is located just beneath these areas and will be stimulated as well. Do reassure your daughter that it takes time and patience for some girls to achieve orgasm initially.

Another important and under-discussed point to make is that sexual behaviour (with yourself or with a partner) doesn't always have to be orgasm focused. It can be highly pleasurable in the absence of an orgasm, for all genders. It's also important to explain that people may orgasm less, more or not at all at different stages in their life and orgasms may change in feeling and intensity. So yes, tell your daughter that it's great to explore, but avoid being too focused on achieving an orgasm – people can feel great sexually with or without!

Topic 5: Sex work

Question from a teacher referring to 15–16 year olds:

> 'In my class some children talk about websites like Only Fans and Pornhub and I know that some of their friends, especially girls, advertise themselves on these kinds of sites. I think this would be a good opportunity to start a discussion about sex work and sex workers. Are they too young for this?'

If they're talking about these kinds of websites and, perhaps, using them we think you're absolutely right to introduce this topic. This would be a great opportunity to challenge their ideas and check their knowledge. But do be aware that for you as a teacher, these debates will be full of personal values. It is, therefore, important to prepare for your lesson by reflecting on your own opinions and values.

To begin the lesson you might want to propose that sex work, regardless of whether it involves being paid for physically performing sexual behaviours on a client or portraying sexual imagery online or in movies, can be considered just a job, with a client paying for a service provided by another person. It will be interesting for you to explore your students' perceptions of this statement and whether they agree or whether their position is more value laden or perhaps whether they consider law and ethics. For example, in many countries sex work is illegal which makes sex workers very vulnerable as they have no legal rights or protection, so in that sense some members in your group may regard it not as a job but as exploitation. Others, however, may believe that it is an individual's right to choose how they earn a living and that this statement is correct.

In our experience, these kinds of debates can become quite heated, so you may wish to go on to encourage the students to research some data about sex work, for example whether there are regions or countries where there are a higher percentage of sex workers and why that may be. Next, you could ask the group to research why someone may do this work. Potential reasons may be: economic, force or it may be a voluntary choice. Try to avoid presenting your personal opinions as facts and, instead, keep the discussion factual. You could also ask the students to search for legal issues around sex work, for example is prostitution legal in your country? Is there a minimum age for working on porn sites and sites like Only Fans?

Once you have addressed these facts, you can proceed to the value-building part of the discussion. Your students could discuss their personal opinions about sex work in small groups and after 10–15 minutes they could summarize their opinions in a few sentences, anonymously, on paper. You could then use these statements as the basis for a debate and you could also add in a further statement such as 'In some countries like Sweden, the law says the sex worker is not to be criminalized but the client is. Therefore, when a client is caught, the client gets a penalty not the sex worker. What do you think of this law?' Finally, you could summarize the discussion by emphasizing that whatever the opinion is about sex workers, they should never be stigmatized; whatever the opinion, every person deserves respect.

Parents and carers may handle these discussions slightly differently as you may wish to convey your family values in your answers. If so, we suggest that you use a similar strategy to the one above but you could also include some debate concerning your personal values. But do emphasize that regardless of your personal views, your child should avoid stigmatizing people because of their work.

Topic 6: Teenage sex under your roof?

Question from a parent:

> 'My 16 year old son has been going out with a girl, who is also
> 16, for 18 months. They are quite close and see each other every
> day at school and after school they do homework together either
> at her house or ours. In our house they go to my son's bedroom.
> Recently they've begun to close the bedroom door and they are
> very quiet, then when they reappear, they are giggly and the girl-
> friend rushes to leave. So, yesterday I went upstairs with a drink
> for them. I knocked on the door and opened it to find them lying
> on his bed, with his girlfriend on top of him half naked. I was
> so shocked, I left immediately saying nothing, and a while later
> they came downstairs and she left right away without saying
> goodbye to me. I am still in shock and very worried as I don't
> want them to become parents at this age. What should I do?'

Having a steady relationship and being in love is the main
reason why young people decide to have sex.[1] So, given their
ages and after 18 months of being together, we're not surprised
that your son and his girlfriend are experimenting sexually and,
equally, if they've decided to have intercourse this would be no
surprise to us either. However, we appreciate that as a parent
this can be a challenging time.

Research has shown significant cultural differences in parents' attitudes towards their adolescent children's romantic
relationships.[2] Dutch parents tend to be accepting of their
teenagers' relationships and prefer their children to have sex
in their own home as it is considered a safer option than other
places where young people may have sex such as parks, beaches,
cars and at parties. However, we know that this is certainly
not an accepted position in other countries, with many parents
insisting that young people keep the bedroom door open if they
have partners over.

Our belief is that parents need to appreciate that young

people have sexual feelings and desires and that they are capable of making well-informed decisions, but at 16 they also need guidance. If parents prevent their teenager from having sex in their own room, they will simply choose another place which could be riskier. Additionally, and just as importantly, a 'ban' is likely to lead to a lack of communication between the adolescent and their parent(s)/carer(s), meaning that the parent won't have any opportunities to guide their child. So, in relation to this question, as a parent your role is to help your child determine whether this is what they want, that they understand the implications and to help them minimize the risks. So, we would advise you to have a conversation about these issues. The example below may be helpful:

> Parent: 'I just wanted to say that I'm sorry for barging into your room the other day. I know what I saw was private, but I'd like to talk about it with you. Is that OK?'

> Son: 'OK, what do you want to know?'

> Parent: 'I don't need to know what you were doing, but I just want to check that you are sure you both want the same thing. Remember the conversation we had about consent? I just want to check that neither of you are feeling pressured?'

> Son: 'Yes, mum, we both want it. And it's not what you think, we're not having sex. But that might come soon, because we're both ready for it. We've talked about it.'

> Parent: 'That's fine. If you're ready to have sex, I really want you to do it safely. Have you discussed this too?

> Son: 'No, not yet. I know she's using the pill but I think we'll need to use condoms too. We'll just have to get them when we're really ready. I don't know when.'

> Parent: 'Can I suggest something? I'm not rushing you but would you let me buy condoms for you until you're 18, because I'm

still responsible for your health as your mum? I'll put them in the blue vase in the bathroom.'

Son: *'Thanks mum. I really appreciate that.'*

Topic 7: Online relationships

Question from a teacher:

'A few of my students are having romantic relationships online. One of the boys in my class told me that he has a boyfriend who he met via social media and they are absolutely in love. Every evening they are online for at least two hours using the webcam and they message and send photos to each other during the day. What kind of things should we be discussing in class about safety?'

The internet connects us with the world. Meeting friends and starting romantic relationships online is as normal for young people as talking on the phone to boyfriends and girlfriends was for their parents when they were young. The internet has become an additional, and for some a preferred, arena to meet others and stay connected, and increasingly young people are using social media to meet people for romantic and/or sexual relationships. Research[3] also shows that homo- or bisexual young people use the internet and dating apps more than heterosexual young people of the same age. Homo-/bisexual young people also use sexting more than heterosexual young people of the same age.[4] Consequently, homo-/bisexual young people also report more negative experiences with sexting than their heterosexual counterparts.

Your student has found a boyfriend on the internet and seems to be in love. This is happy news and it should be celebrated in the same way as it would be if they had met in a traditional context. At this stage they may or may not have a sexual relationship but they may share nude pictures or masturbate in front of the webcam. While it's great that your student is happy, you're right to have some concerns about safety as everything that people do and post on the internet stays there and is potentially accessible to others. It is, therefore, worth revisiting the fundamental aspects of internet safety and consent with your students.

Topic 8: Sexual assault

Question from a parent:

'My 15 year old daughter was sexually assaulted a few months ago at a friend's house during a party. She has only just told me and I'm really shocked. She was a bit drunk and got talking to a boy who she danced with. At the end of the evening he gently pulled her into the bathroom to kiss her. She said she wanted to be kissed and found it exciting to be in the bathroom with him. But then he wanted to do more, she objected and told him to stop and initially he did and continued to just kiss, but then he started to touch her again and finally penetrated her with his fingers. This was not what she wanted or expected. This was her first sexual encounter. She has felt ashamed since it happened and hasn't told anyone until now. She has just tried to continue with her life as usual. When she told me what happened she tried to dismiss the incident as "it just happened mum, it's my fault, I went into the bathroom with him, so let's forget it". What can I do?'

Any sexual situation that occurs against an individual's will can be considered sexual harassment or sexual abuse. While every case of sexual harassment or sexual abuse is absolutely wrong and unacceptable, the consequences for the young person will vary depending upon the nature of the experience (e.g. what happened, the situation, relationship with perpetrator), personal characteristics of the victim (e.g. coping strategies, age, personal skills), characteristics of the family (e.g. concurrent stressful events experienced by the family, quality of parent-child relationship, family functioning) and sources of support (e.g. reaction of family and friends to disclosure, family and peer group support, professional support).

Many experts believe that parental support is an important factor in helping sexually abused children adjust following abuse and in reducing the risk of longer term impacts, regardless of the nature of the abuse experienced. Coping strategies vary depending upon the personality of the victim as well. In your case, your daughter is finding her own way to deal with her emotions and memories. Time will tell whether this specific strategy works for her, but knowing that you are there to support her will, most likely, be a huge help. So tell her this and make sure that you also tell her that what happened was absolutely not her fault. She may blame herself because she was a bit drunk, or because she kissed him, or danced with him, or didn't say no firmly enough – but none of these things is a reason for her to blame herself. Blame can only be attributed to the person who didn't ensure that they had the other person's consent to engage in a sexual act.

It would be wise to ask for professional support for you as a mother and, in time, for your daughter as soon as she is open to it. Although 'just forgetting' what happened may work for now, in the longer term some people experience psychological consequences such as depression, anxiety disorder and post-traumatic stress disorder if the underlying issue isn't addressed. With your support, coupled with professional support, your daughter has the potential to learn from this experience and go on to develop positive relationships.

Topic 9: Talking about genders

Question from a parent:

'My daughter's classmate told her that she thinks she is trans and it seems that my daughter doesn't understand what her classmate means. What can I tell her and which terms should I use?'

It's a good idea to talk with your daughter about gender diversity in its broadest sense. Here are some key points and language that you may find useful:

- The term 'sex' is usually used to refer to biological sex, meaning that a person is male if they have a penis or female if they have a vagina. However, some people have non-distinguishing genitals or have both a penis and a vagina, making traditional definitions problematic. Others define 'sex' by an individual's chromosomes (XX for females and XY for males) but this leaves some people confused if they are neither XX nor XY.

- Gender is different to 'sex' because it is a socially constructed term. Traditional communities may only refer to women/girls and men/boys and they may try to determine the roles that men and women are supposed to conform to. However, increasingly gender diversity, where people are no longer expected to conform to the male and female binaries, is becoming accepted with people choosing to look and behave in the way they choose.

- Cisgender describes people who feel the same gender as the sex assigned to them biologically. For example, people born with a vagina, clitoris and vulva who consider themselves a woman. Or people born with a penis who feel like a boy or a man.

- Trans people feel that they are a different gender to the one given to them at birth. Unlike cis people, trans people don't feel the same gender as their biological sex. A trans man might want to be called 'he/him' and a trans woman might prefer being called 'she/her', although some trans people also prefer to use a non-binary pronoun such as 'they/them'.

- Some trans people decide to go into transition which means they go through a medical and psychological process to adapt their body to become more the gender they feel they are. This may involve the use of hormones and surgery. This is possible for children and adolescents, although different countries have different laws and guidelines concerning what age the process of transition can start.

- Intersex people are born with a combination of male and female biological traits, including a natural variation in hormones, reproductive or sexual organs that don't fit the typical definitions of female or male, or cells with a mixture of XX and XY chromosomes. Some children and their parents are not aware of these differences until adolescence or even later, when certain pubertal changes do not become apparent. For others, being intersex is clear at birth if the external genitals are not as expected.

- Non-binary people are people who do not want to be put in fixed binary genders – man/woman or male/female. Sometimes non-binary people call themselves 'genderqueer' which includes people who have no gender, two or more genders or who are fluid about their gender. Some non-binary people prefer to use or to be called a non-binary pronoun like 'they/them'.

It may also be worth highlighting that it's not for other people to judge how others should look or be labelled; this is always the individual's personal right and decision. We have listed some wonderful websites below where you and your daughter can look for more information about gender, sex and all the other terms used here:

- www.bishuk.com/about-you/sex-and-gender (for young people, parents and teachers)

- www.stonewall.org.uk (for young people and adults)

- www.wikihow.com/Respect-a-Transgender-Person (for young people and adults)

- www.mermaidsuk.org.uk (for gender diverse kids and adolescents and their families).

Topic 10: Female genital mutilation

Question from a teacher:

'I want to discuss female genital mutilation (FGM) with my class because I think it's an important aspect of sexuality education. My school has a diverse population and I'm mindful that I need to handle the discussions sensitively as some of the girls or their families may have been affected by FGM. How could I go about this?'

We agree that discussing FGM in class could be very helpful to your students but we also acknowledge that it can be a challenging conversation that can become very value-based and emotional. As you point out, when discussing FGM in the classroom, it's important to be mindful that at least one girl in your class is likely to have had direct or indirect experience of FGM. Whilst the illegal nature of FGM needs to be explained, great care needs to be taken when discussing what FGM is and what its potential impacts may be. FGM can have lifelong consequences for a girl, physically, mentally and sexually. By judging FGM in general, a student may feel personally attacked if she has experienced FGM. Our suggestion is to ask a health care worker with experience in working with women with FGM to contribute to your session.

The most helpful strategy we've found in our training is to make a distinction between facts and opinions/values. You could begin with outlining what FGM is, how common it is in your city or country, reasons behind FGM, what the WHO website says about it and what the law in your country is regarding FGM. Key facts that you may wish to address are:

- FGM is illegal in many western and non-western countries.

- There are many different forms of FGM; the most extreme method involves the removal of the glans of the clitoris and the inner labia (and sometimes also the outer lips) and closing the rest of the vulval tissue around the clitoris, leaving an opening for the vagina for menstruation and penetration during sexual intercourse. Less invasive methods are used in 'symbolic circumcision', which may involve a small incision in the hood covering the top of the clitoris.

- FGM is often carried out in unclean conditions, without analgesia, which can have lifetime consequences, both physically and mentally (see www.who.int/news-room/fact-sheets/detail/female-genital-mutilation).

- According to the WHO, all forms of FGM are harmful practices for women.

- FGM is recognized internationally as a violation of the human rights of girls and women. It reflects deep-rooted inequality between the sexes, and constitutes an extreme form of discrimination against women. It is nearly always carried out on minors and is a violation of the rights of children. The practice also violates a person's rights to health, security and physical integrity, the right to be free from torture and cruel, inhuman or degrading treatment, and the right to life when the procedure results in death.[5]

Chapter 8

Late adolescence (16–18+ years)

WHAT ADULTS WANT TO KNOW

What's it like to be 16–18?

The majority of young people in this age group will have reached the end of puberty, meaning that the rapid physical changes are over, although they will continue to grow and develop until their early 20s, but at a more moderate pace. Brain development is ongoing with the prefrontal cortex continuing to develop until around the age of 25. At this stage, the prefrontal cortex is flexible and can function better than an adult's when given tasks that they consider useful and highly important[1] (see also Chapter 4). Most young people are increasingly able to concentrate at this stage and they are able to engage in verbal debates at an adult level with their peers, parents and teachers. They are now able to make informed choices, but are not yet fully able to understand the possible consequences of their choices. If, for instance, they have an important exam in a few days and should concentrate on their revision but they get an invitation for a spontaneous party, some of them will abandon their studies to go to the party (although others might continue to concentrate on their exam). Although they are aware of the exam, the ones who go will argue that they will compensate for the lost time the following day with some extra study, without realizing that they may have a hangover, feel sleepy and totally unfocused the following day.

Young people of this age often still feel a need to experience new situations, to experiment and to seek out excitement. Some adults consider this behaviour risky and find it a worrying stage. For young people though it is the rewards of adventure and excitement that attract and trigger them, not the possible risks that they are likely to encounter. Some adolescents may think in an 'egocentric' way and feel that they are the centre of the world. But to call them 'egocentric' would be incorrect because lots of young people at this age are highly concerned and involved in many social topics like climate change and human rights. Their self-esteem is still developing and the influence of peer pressure is beginning to decrease. At this stage young people generally feel that they are capable of looking after themselves and strive for independence, which can sometimes lead to conflict with parents and carers.

At the upper end of the age range that this chapter addresses, 18 year olds are legally considered adults in the majority of countries. However, their brains continue to develop until their mid-20s, meaning that several crucial functions like memory, planning, attention, self-reflection and the skill to regulate thought, emotions and empathy are yet to be fully developed.[2] However, they have great capacity to have discussions with adults, in formulating their arguments on a specific standpoint, in making long-term plans and making independent decisions. Throughout this stage, the role of the carer and parent gradually changes, moving from guider and teacher to companion, supporter and hopefully someone who inspires. Increasingly, at this stage young people are capable of making their own decisions and may not always share them with their loved ones, and equally, they may not want to hear their loved ones' opinions.

Throughout this chapter, as with the previous two, we have

taken the stage of development into account, as well as the international guidance outlined in Chapter 6 and the research for this book, to answer several questions asked by parents, carers and professionals. We hope you find the discussions helpful.

Topic 1: Sexual pleasure

Question from a parent:

> 'My daughter of 17 is worried because her girlfriend has recently told her that she finds their sex-life dull. How can I tell her how to make it more pleasurable without being too explicit?'

Before we answer your question, a quick well done – it's great that your daughter can talk to you in this way! Our first bit of advice is to tell her that what is called 'dull' for one person could be exciting for another. Reassure your daughter that any sexual relationship can become 'dull' in the eyes of one or both partners and there are some general principles that can be applied to make sexual behaviour more pleasurable, without you having to go into too much detail. Indeed, you'd be doing your daughter a disservice by being too explicit as sexual pleasure is something personal and young people need to discover for themselves through experience what they find pleasurable or not.

It may be helpful to explain to your daughter that, contrary to popular belief, sex is much more than 'vaginal penetration', with a finger, a dildo or, in a hetero relationship, a penis. Sexual pleasure can come from just touching, caressing, stroking the skin and stimulating each other's genitals to give a pleasurable feeling. Fingers, hands and tongues can play important roles in many creative ways to reach sexual pleasure for both partners in hetero and non-heterosexual relationships.

Other important points to make are that sexual pleasure is about more than just reaching orgasm. As with anything else in life, sexual pleasure is something that needs to be worked on and goes beyond the physical act because it includes positive feelings, emotions and fantasies. Although practice is often needed, young people can have very satisfying and pleasurable sexual relationships. Equally though, sexual pleasure can be experienced alone. Pleasurable sex is strongly related to safer sex because if sex is safe and consensual, it's easier to relax, be curious and creative. Clear communication, a positive self-image, self-confidence, knowing what you like and don't like, mutual respect, trust, checking for each other's 'yeses' and 'nos', kindness and a lack of force or pressure can all lead to greater sexual pleasure. Finally, as we have said earlier, pleasure and dull are both personal concepts. Encourage your daughter to talk with her girlfriend about what they both find nice, exciting and enjoyable to do in their sexual relationship. What is the part the girlfriend considers dull and how can they both contribute to change this part into a more exciting experience?

By talking openly with your daughter and encouraging her to communicate with her girlfriend, she will be better prepared to make her sexual relationship enjoyable. As long as your daughter is aware of these principles, she'll find her own way in this exciting journey together with her girlfriend. Or they may find, with time, that they have different needs and go their separate ways.

Topic 2: Experimenting with sexuality: Hetero? Gay? Lesbian? Bisexual?

Question from a teacher:

'In my class of 17/18 year olds, I'm surprised to see how my students are experimenting with their sexual orientation. Some have same-sex relationships and, a few months later, some of them have heterosexual relationships. What's happening?'

This kind of experimentation is quite common during adolescence because young people are searching for their sexual orientation and trying to discover what they like and don't like. For some, their sexual orientation will have been clear from a young age and they might not need to experiment, but others will because they are less certain and need to explore their sexual identity. Experimentation may lead to several different sexual partners in quick succession or concurrently. This doesn't have to be risky as long as everyone is engaging safely and consensually, although it must be acknowledged that research shows that a higher number of different partners can lead to a greater risk of non-consensual experiences and sexually transmitted infections.[3] In terms of the benefits, experimenting sexually can give young people more knowledge about their desires and boundaries but it can also lead to disappointments if the partner or the sexual encounter is not as had been hoped for.

In terms of your response to your students, your reactions are likely to be shaped by your personal values and it is important for you to be clear with them that these are your values rather than facts. Factual information that would be useful to them includes consent, the use of safe contraception and some of the principles regarding sexual pleasure outlined in topic 1.

Topic 3: Designer vulva

Question from a parent:

> 'My daughter, Emma, will be 18 next month. For her birthday, Emma wants her labia operated on because she says they are too long and they hurt her when cycling and doing sport. I'm really not keen on paying for this. I've heard about the "designer vulva" and I just don't get it. Any suggestions for how I handle this please?'

Insecurity or dissatisfaction with how they look is very common among young people at this stage. They may be unhappy with their bodyweight, their face, their nose, the size of their breasts, hips, legs, arms, buttocks, the size or appearance of their genitals, their skin... in fact any part of themselves. Often they compare themselves with airbrushed images on social media which are unrealistic, and in the case of genitals some will only see others' genitals in porn which are often modified digitally or surgically.

With regards to vulva surgery, also known as labia surgery or labiaplasty, the American College of Obstetricians and Gynecologists (ACOG) and the Royal College of Obstetricians and Gynaecologists (RCOG) have both expressed their concerns about the increase of labiaplasty among teenagers in the USA and the UK. A 40% increase in labiaplasty was seen in US teenage girls from 2015 to 2016.[4]

Most young women requesting labiaplasty say that their longer labia cause them physical discomfort during sports and sexual behaviour. Many also report psychological discomfort because they consider their inner labia abnormal or ugly, leading to low self-esteem and shyness in relation to intimate sexual behaviour. These perceptions may be influenced by teenage girls' exposure to pictures of female vulvas on social media, without knowing that these are digitally modified and not real at all. Similarly, in porn, participants' genitals are highly digitally adapted and this can make female viewers insecure and uncomfortable about their own vulvas. This is particularly so among young women who usually lack knowledge of the normal anatomy of the vulva and, of course, this can also have a negative impact upon boys' perceptions of 'normality'.

In relation to what to say to Emma, it would be a good idea to discuss the normal anatomy of the female vulva from baby girl to female adult. Many people don't know that baby girls have 'closed' vulvas, meaning that the outer lips of the vulva are bigger than the inner lips and usually fold themselves around the shorter inner lips. Between the ages of 8 and 10 years, the form of the vulva slowly changes from that of a baby towards a more adult form, due to hormonal changes. The vulva lips (labia) become bigger and change in colour. In most girls, the inner lips lengthen and they are often of uneven length. The growth of the vulval lips serves an important function since the additional tissue with its sensitive nerves is responsible for pleasure during sexual behaviour. So, if a woman or girl has her inner lips shortened, she may compromise the potential for sexual pleasure now and later in her life.

To help Emma understand the unique nature of the vulva, it may be helpful for her to look at the website 'The Vulva Gallery' (www.thevulvagallery.com) by female artist Hilde Atalanta. Hilde asked hundreds of women to send in a picture of their vulva which she then copied and painted for her website and book. Your daughter will clearly see that every vulva is different and hopefully she will see that her vulva is normal.

In relation to the discomfort that Emma is experiencing, this may be caused by:

- shaving the outer labia too often
- washing the vulva too often, especially with soap or other detergents
- wearing panties that are too tight
- tightening of the pelvic floor muscles
- wearing jeans or other seamed trousers when cycling and doing sport.

So, we would also advise that she considers this advice, and if after making appropriate changes she is still uncomfortable it would be sensible for her to visit her family doctor so that other causes of discomfort such as thrush (vulvovaginal candidiasis) can be checked for and, if appropriate, treated.

Topic 4: Asexuality

Question from a teacher:

'An 18 year old girl in my class recently approached me for guid-ance. She is very fashionable, appears confident and is very pop-ular with both the boys and girls. She is concerned that she has never experienced any sexual feelings, and when she listens to her classmates' steamy discussions about their sexual experiences, she feels lonely, isolated and abnormal. She has no desire to be or become sexual. She has had several short romantic relationships, with boys as well as with girls, which were enjoyable until they became sexual. She didn't enjoy kissing or touching or being touched. She did enjoy the hugging stage, but nothing more than this. She said that she really needs and desires intimacy, but not sex. She has recently discovered the term asexual and wondered if this applies to her. I am unfamiliar with this term. What does it mean?'

In relationships and sexuality education the focus is often on the inevitability of sexual experiences for young people and the fact that some young people and adults have no need or desire for any sexual experience can be overlooked. However, we know that some people don't feel comfortable with physical intimacy and may avoid romantic relationships because they know that an expectation of sexual behaviour is likely.

Generally in western societies, age 15–25 is considered the period when people experience their greatest sexual drive and it can be very difficult for a young person who doesn't experience the same high sexual desires as their peers, or indeed no sexual desire at all. It can make young people feel abnormal and lonely and some may try to make themselves feel normal by engaging in sexual relationships without having any physical desire or by having sex when drunk or intoxicated with drugs. But this rarely achieves what the young person hoped for, with young people describing feeling unfulfilled, disappointed and/or dirty afterwards.

Some people call this asexuality. For some, asexuality is perceived as a disorder which can further contribute to people's sense of 'abnormality'. Others have long considered asexuality as a consequence of some earlier trauma, such as sexual abuse or sexual violence. By framing asexuality in this way, the inference is that it is treatable. But nowadays, increasingly asexuality is perceived as just one of many existing possible sexual identities. Some people who have no sexual desire don't want to be labelled asexual or, indeed, any other label, because of the associated stigma. Equally, others don't want to see it as a disorder, and perceive it as simply a state of being that they don't have any problem with.

Our preference is to avoid labels and, instead, we would advise that you simply show understanding and respect for your student's personal perspectives and wishes concerning sexuality. Also, if you are involved in any aspect of the group's relationships and sexuality education, it would be helpful to explain that everyone is different and some young people won't be interested in sex or have any desire to have sexual relationships. Indeed, we would recommend that this is an integral part of all discussions regarding relationships and sexuality education.

As this young person has explained, people who don't desire sex may desire intimacy or physical closeness. However, this may differ and it's important to avoid generalizations. It should not be assumed that people with no sexual desires have always experienced a trauma or have been abused. For some this may be the case but for others it won't be. Equally, some people may always feel this way, but for others it is only temporary. Regardless of any potential 'cause', whether these feelings are temporary or not and whether a person may or may not desire alternative forms of closeness, it's important that you accept this young person's account as one of the many diverse orientations and possibilities of sexuality in human beings, without judging it as something negative.

Topic 5: Festivals and holidays

Question from a parent:

> 'This summer my 17 year old will be going to a three-day music festival with his friends. There'll be around 100,000 young people there with minimal supervision. We're worried about him going but understand that we need to let him grow up. There will be alcohol and illicit drugs and, of course, the opportunity for sex. He knows the risks of unprotected intercourse, so the knowledge is there and we hope he will be smart enough to make responsible decisions. Unfortunately, he doesn't want to talk about contraception with me, but I really don't want him coming home with an STI or as a young father. Do you have any advice for me please?'

This is a very common situation for carers and parents of 16–18 year olds. As we discussed in Chapter 1, some young people will have already consumed alcohol, tobacco and drugs by this age so experimental behaviour has already begun, and going to festivals or on holidays with friends, without parents, is part of this. Our advice is to be sure that your son has enough knowledge about protecting himself and others against STIs and unplanned pregnancies, that he knows about consent and peer pressure and that he is willing and able to take his own health-related decisions. And finally, give him a pack of condoms to put in his bag, even though he is likely to object! Your parting message could be: 'Even if you don't need them, one of your friends might. And if you just bring them home that's fine too.' By saying something like this, you'll show your son that you trust him and, although he may not show it, he'll appreciate it!

Topic 6: Transactional sex

Question from a teacher:

> *'In my class of 17–18 year olds, several boys and girls are openly acknowledging that they have sex just to get things like a new mobile phone or a ticket for a pop concert. One girl came into school the other day with a new Gucci bag and told the other girls she got it from her new boyfriend as a gift for sex. I have tried to talk to them about the importance of love in relationships but it seemed not to register. What can I do?'*

Trading sex in return for personal gain is nothing new. Some people make a living from it, some are forced to do it for security, for example sex for rent, and others do it because they want something such as a Gucci handbag. Traditionally, sex has been seen as something sacred that should be reserved for marriage or at least for situations where people are in love. These are western norms, based on religious foundations. However, norms and values are bound by culture, time and context, so as time and context change, norms and values change too. Young people's sexual norms are changing rapidly, as reflected in their music, literature and media, but, again, this is nothing new. For example, the 'free sex' of the 1970s 'hippie generation' was shocking for parents and other adults at that time, but norms are dynamic and, as we can see today, many of the '70s hippies' are now in their seventies and are traditional (grand)mothers or (grand)fathers with steady relationships who no longer want the free-sex society or community which they once celebrated. However, although norms change with time, some influences remain, for example since the 1970s many parents have allowed their children to experiment with several sexual partners during their adolescence and young adulthood until they decide to marry. Another influence is that cohabitation outside of marriage is widely accepted although it was disapproved of just a few generations ago. In fact in the USA and the UK around half of children are born outside marriage, indicating that marriage is no longer necessarily the norm as a way to organize a family. And so, inevitably, today's generation of young people have their own ideas about sex. According to research,[5] the main reasons young people have sex are because:

- they are in love
- they consider sex to be part of being in a relationship
- curiosity
- they feel sexually aroused
- they want to have the experience
- everyone else has done it.

Somewhere far below these six main reasons is one which said: 'because I wanted to get something done', with this applying to just a small percentage of respondents.

As an educator your role is concerned with helping young people to develop their own values, even if they are at odds with your own. Adolescents are more willing to listen to adults they admire and have a good relationship with, and encouraging these kinds of discussions in which you all share your ideas and values about sexuality is valuable and important. Although it might seem that they are ignoring you or they may suggest that you are out of touch, your input may help some of the students evaluate what they want to get out of sexual relationships. If you want to, you can tell them your personal values, but only if you are clear that these are your personal values and that everyone is free to have their own. If you think love is an important part of sexual pleasure you can explain this to them. For some of your students this might open them up to new ideas, but it would be wrong to assert that sex without love could never be pleasurable.

Topic 7: Sexual harassment

Question from a parent:

'My child will leave school soon to go to university and I'm worried that they aren't sufficiently prepared to face the challenges of the adult world. I've heard lots of stories about students who have faced sexual harassment and abuse on university campuses. Am I worrying too much or is this a reality for them?'

Studies show that you are right about sexual harassment on university campuses internationally and the Higher Education Policy Institute recently published a report on this.[6] Only a small proportion of students in this poll felt that their prior education had prepared them for the reality of sex and relationships in higher education (6%) and a majority of the students thought that it should be compulsory to pass a sexual consent assessment before entering higher education. So, discussing consent, sexuality, risk minimization and what to do if sexual harassment occurs is a necessary part of preparing your child for stepping into the life of an undergraduate. Another important issue to discuss is what is sometimes called 'street harassment' or 'street intimidation', where (mainly) boys shout remarks at girls as they pass by in the street. Typically, these remarks are sexist, sexual and/or derogatory. Boys should know that this kind of behaviour can be offensive and intimidating for girls. And girls should know that they don't have to accept this behaviour.

If you provide this input before your child leaves home, you will be providing them with an invaluable parting gift. Resources that you could use include:

- For the UK:
  - www.brook.org.uk
  - www.bishtraining.com by Justin Hancock

- For Australia:

    - Website of Legal Services Commission of South Australia (www.lsc.sa.gov.au) for lots of factsheets

    - *Talk Soon, Talk Often*

- For the USA:

    - 'Consent is as easy as Fries' on the website of Planned Parenthood

    - 'Consent' on the website of Advocates for Youth

Topic 8: Asserting boundaries

Question from a teacher:

> *'In preparation for my relationships and sexuality education lessons, I asked students to tell me what they wanted from the lesson, using an anonymous questionnaire. A recurring theme was how to say "no" or "not yet" to boyfriends or girlfriends without risking losing them. I don't really know how to advise them, what would you suggest?'*

This can be a big challenge for young, and not so young, people. Relationships can make people feel wanted, admired, appreciated and special. And, of course, more often than not people make a strong emotional investment in relationships and really like or love their partners. Objecting to the other's sexual advances can, therefore, feel risky because of the fear of rejection and all of the losses that this could bring. In addition, it is very easy to get carried away by the situation, with previously well thought through principles about what is a 'yes' and what is a definite 'no' flying out the window!

It takes real self-confidence for a young person to object to sexual advances that will cross a line that they are not ready to cross. The outcome is unknown and unpredictable, with young people often assuming that the reaction will be negative. The reaction may be one of understanding, relief or agreement, but indignation, outrage, anger or ridicule are often anticipated. It is this point that can form the basis of discussions in class, with the aim of breaking down and challenging such assumptions.

While being sensitive to the fluidity of gender and varying sexual orientations, you could begin the discussion by asking the young people to get into small groups and debate stereotypical statements, such as:

- If boys aren't pushy sexually, they risk being viewed as abnormal.

- If a young person doesn't agree to sex they will be considered prudish.

- Rejecting sexual advances will lead to a break up.

- Girls are the 'gatekeepers' for intercourse.

- If a girl says yes to sex or takes the first step she'll be seen as a slut.

- Saying no to sex, in a kind way, is perfectly alright.

You could ask the young people to write down their reactions to these statements anonymously. You could also invite them to write down how they would react to someone saying 'no' to them and whether it would lead to them ending the relationship. You could then use these written responses to facilitate an anonymized plenary discussion. In our experience, the consensus is generally that young people disagree with stereotypical assumptions and are, generally, respectful of other people's wishes. Exploring whether this is a surprise to the class would be helpful too.

Following this, it's important to revisit the concept of 'consent'. At this stage, an applied discussion is appropriate.

Misunderstandings, nervousness regarding how to object or feeling that it is too late to object because the other person is in a state of heightened sexual arousal (which is no reason not to object) can be (partly) avoided if both partners are used to asking for consent. Encourage the class to develop statements that they could use to seek consent. Examples may be: *'I love your kisses. Shall we go to the next step or do you want to stop?'*; or: *'I love your kisses; I'd love to do more. How about you? It's OK if you want to wait or think about it.'* They may find it awkward at first but this is an invaluable exercise and can lead to a lot of fun.

Chapter 9

'Is this OK?'

'I saw a 13 year old pupil French kissing her 14 year old boyfriend, is that OK?'

'A 17 year old boy in my class has sent a nude picture of himself to his boyfriend, is that OK?'

These kinds of questions come up repeatedly during our training sessions with adults on relationships and sexuality education because it isn't always easy to establish what sexual behaviour is acceptable and what isn't. People often have different opinions, and without any objective criteria it's almost impossible to decide who is right. Importantly, with such uncertainty, it's also difficult to know how or whether to intervene.

In this chapter we explore how we can determine what's acceptable and unacceptable sexual behaviour, using objective criteria developed by Erika Frans and Sensoa called the Flag System. Although the Flag System was primarily developed for professionals, we have found that it can also be helpful for parents, carers and even adolescents themselves. Throughout the chapter we will outline the system and discuss how you can use it, using practical examples. To obtain the full resource please see the note[1] in the endnotes section at the back of this book.

The Flag System's aims

The Flag System is designed to enable professionals to assess what is acceptable and unacceptable sexual behaviour in children and young people aged 0–18 years. The system gives objective criteria based on research to develop our judgement in a more objective way and tries to enable users to suspend their instinctive reactions which may cloud objectivity. The system also suggests appropriate responses with the aim of promoting healthy sexual development.

As we have discussed in the previous chapters, we observe sexual behaviour with children and adolescents in all kinds of different contexts, so we are likely to see sexual behaviour at home, in school, sport clubs, parks and wherever else young people spend their time. In most countries the general belief is that parents are entitled to deal with this behaviour in the way they see fit but professionals need to be able to clearly communicate and justify their response to parents and colleagues and demonstrate consistency. For this reason the Flag System is now widely used by professionals across Europe who work in a variety of settings, such as care, education, social work and sport, to discuss sexually (un)acceptable behaviour with co-workers, management, parents, carers and with the children and young people themselves. Increasingly it is also being used by parents because they find it a useful guide.

The Flag System is designed to provide professionals with answers to important questions such as:

- How do we know what is OK and what isn't?

- How should we judge?

- How should we respond?

It aims to contribute to children's and adolescents' healthy sexual development and to prevent sexual coercion. Using the

Flag System creates room for positive sexual development and behaviour; simply banning sexual behaviour is never a solution.

How it works

Consider the following behaviours that young people might exhibit:

Two 13 year old girls in a bedroom, caressing one another between and over their thighs. They are enjoying it.

A father walking in on his 16 year old son and his 17 year old girlfriend, who are naked in bed. They are both enjoying it. There are condoms on the bedside table.

A 15 year old girl having anal sex with her boyfriend. She has consented to it but doesn't like it. She agrees to it because she doesn't want to lose her boyfriend.

Two 16 year olds are having oral sex in the bushes. They both like it.

Here's an exercise for you:

- Make a judgement regarding how harmful the above behaviours are.

- Think through how you came to this judgement.

It's likely that your reaction was based on an instinctive response and, perhaps, some past experience or some understandings regarding what you consider appropriate behaviour at different stages of development. The Flag System aims to enable users to go beyond an instinctive response by providing six objective criteria that can be used to assess which behaviours are OK and which aren't. Please note that these descriptions are just a short overview; if you want to learn more we recommend you read the full Sensoa Flag System.[2]

The first criterion is **mutual consent**, which means mutual agreement. Both parties must give their full and conscious permission. If one party leaves the other in any uncertainty, misleads, cheats or overwhelms the other, consent cannot be assumed. The difficulty with this criterion is that consent is often given non-verbally and people can change their minds once they are engaged in the situation. This is something both parties have to be mindful of. So adolescents need to be taught to interpret signals clearly and give clear signals themselves. And of course, they need to be taught to stop if the other party changes their mind, whether this is indicated verbally or non-verbally. This is also addressed in Chapters 5–8.

The second criterion is **voluntary engagement**, which is concerned with the individual's willingness to participate. At first, this criterion might seem similar to mutual consent. However, consent is about giving permission to someone else, voluntary engagement is about what the individual really wants. When a teenager concedes to sexual behaviour that they don't want, there is no voluntary engagement. An example is where a boy touches a girl's breasts in a game of 'truth or dare' and one or both parties are scared to say no. Subtle forms of coercion and force such as persuasion and manipulation can lead to involuntary engagement. You can't always see whether this criterion is met, so you often have to ask questions to ascertain this. It is important to note that only the individual involved in the situation can assess whether their personal participation is really voluntary.

The third criterion is **equality**. Sexual behaviour becomes more pleasurable and more safe when both parties are evenly matched. Both should have equal power within the relationship without being controlled or coerced by the other. So, there should be balance between both parties in terms of age, knowledge, intelligence, power, maturity and status.

The fourth criterion is assessing if the behaviour is **appropriate for the stage of development or age**. The focus here is on determining whether the sexual behaviour that the adolescent exhibits might be expected for his or her age as well as his or her biological, psychological, social and emotional stage of development. This isn't something you can easily see or check, as it requires knowledge about sexual development. Your own experience is not enough to refer to. Chapters 5–8 of this book are very helpful in this regard.

The fifth criterion is checking whether the behaviour is **appropriate within the context**. Healthy sexual behaviour in the wrong context can be shocking or insulting, for example the same sexual behaviour might be acceptable in the privacy of one's bedroom but not in school. In practice, we've found this the most challenging criterion because people have different opinions about what appropriate contexts for sexual behaviour are, with cultural differences often playing a big role. For example two boys holding hands or two teenagers kissing may be considered acceptable in both private and public by some people but others may believe that these should be purely private behaviours. These differences in perspectives can lead to different assessments. Below we will explain how the different perspectives play a role within the Flag System.

The sixth and final criterion is **self-respect or impact**. This criterion promotes the importance of children and adolescents not harming themselves through their behaviours. Sexual behaviour can be harmful physically, psychologically and socially and young people may feel humiliated and get hurt physically and/or emotionally by getting involved in risky situations. In our previous book this criterion was called 'self-respect'. Sensoa recently changed it to 'impact' and we think this makes the meaning of this criterion clearer. In the rest of this chapter we will use the word 'impact'.

Here's a second exercise for you to do:

- Return to the situations we outlined at the beginning of the chapter and apply the six Flag System criteria to determine how harmful you consider these behaviours to be.

- Have your assessments of the situations changed?

Asking yourself questions as to whether the criteria are met is a good way to analyse what's really going on. It helps you to question your emotional or instinctive response and to consider whether you are being too relaxed, overly anxious or reacting too harshly. Checking all the criteria also helps a great deal when discussing the situation with a colleague or partner or of course with the adolescents themselves.

But... in reality, it's unlikely that you will really know all that has happened in a situation, because you may have only witnessed a snapshot or perhaps the situation wasn't clear when you observed it. For example, it's hard to hear whispered exchanges or to know what conversations have occurred through direct messaging on a mobile phone. In this case, it's necessary to ask questions to clarify exactly what happened. Although you will probably experience an array of thoughts and feelings when trying to ascertain the facts, it's important to try not to judge at this time. By suspending your assumptions and putting your emotions aside you're more likely to discover additional information about the situation when talking to the adolescents and, as a result, respond more appropriately.

The four flags

Once you have accurately determined what has happened in a situation (which probably wasn't easy!) you need to assess to what extent the behaviour is either problematic or acceptable. The aim of this assessment is not to judge the participants, but to determine how you should react. The idea is that by adopting a consistent informed response, adolescents will benefit developmentally. They should feel better able to trust the adults in their lives to make reasoned decisions and to give good advice and they should be better able to set and respect boundaries and even use the criteria themselves. Before telling you a little more about appropriate responses, let's first focus on the four flags.

The green flag

If all of the above criteria are met, the behaviour is given a **green flag**. But, if one or more criteria aren't met, the behaviour will warrant a yellow, red or black flag instead. What is important to note here is that it is not the number of criteria that determine if a yellow, red or black flag is given, but it is the degree of unacceptability that is key. In the coming paragraphs this will become clearer.

The yellow flag

Moderately unacceptable behaviour gets a **yellow flag**. An example may be when moderate pressure is used or when the behaviour is not completely appropriate within the context. It's important to realize that 'yellow behaviour' is still quite acceptable in the development of healthy sexual behaviour, because exploration and pushing the boundaries can be a normal part of development.

The red flag

When we come across seriously unacceptable behaviour, we assign a **red flag**. This is applied when one of the first three criteria (mutual consent, voluntary engagement and equality) clearly aren't met. Another example when a red flag applies is when you observe sexual behaviour which is unusual for the age of the adolescent. This type of behaviour could lead to significant mental (or physical) damage or harm. In addition, yellow behaviour that occurs repeatedly, even when addressed, also gets a red flag.

The black flag

A **black flag** is assigned when you come across very seriously unacceptable behaviour. For example, when the sexual contact is forced with threats, aggression or violence, or when there is great inequality between the participants like sexual behaviour between a 40 year old and a teenager. A black flag can also be assigned when the consequences of the behaviour can be extremely damaging, for example when sexual pictures are publicly posted on the internet.

As you might have noticed, it's not about how many criteria are met, but about the level of unacceptable behaviour. When judging the (un)acceptability of a situation, the Flag System focuses on how harmful the situation is for the participants. It is not about adults judging that adolescents are simply too young to be involved in sexual behaviour. The Flag System states that a dilemma regarding appropriateness within a certain context can shift the colour of the flag by only one, so it can shift from green to yellow, but not from green to red. For example, if we return to the boys holding hands in public, if all other criteria are met, this can be a green flag situation, but, if you consider this inappropriate behaviour in this context, it might become a yellow flag situation. However, you can't assign a red or a black flag just because you think the context isn't right. So there is some room for personal opinions in the Flag System, although this is deliberately limited because the system was developed to promote objectivity among professionals. As we have said earlier in the book, parents have more freedom to use their personal values in dealing with sexual behaviour.

How to respond

Green flag behaviours should be given space as they are part of healthy sexual development. With these types of behaviours you don't always have to react immediately and you may consciously choose not to react at all. Sometimes though it's good to respond because young people can learn from your response, so you may choose to name what you saw and perhaps use it to prompt a conversation. Examples might be:

'It's OK to explore each other's bodies as long as you both like it. Remember that you shouldn't feel pressured though. Just let me know if you want a chat.'

'How did you find flirting with her online?'

'It's nice to see that you're happy with how your body is changing. How do you feel about how you look?'

'It's very normal to be curious about these topics, but if you want to talk about anything with me just let me know.'

By doing this, adults can help adolescents learn to talk about sexual behaviour. It also shows them that adults are happy to talk about these kinds of things with them and that they are there for them if they have any questions or concerns.

When a yellow, red or black flag is assigned, you should

immediately stop the behaviour. With yellow behaviour shown by young children, this can sometimes be achieved by distracting a child; with teenagers it's better to name the behaviour and explain which boundary is being crossed and what they can do differently. Some examples are:

When a 13 year old boy tries to persuade a girl to kiss him, her kiss isn't truly voluntary.

> 'You are putting pressure on the girl to kiss you. What do you think will happen? What could go wrong? It is OK to ask for a kiss if you want one, but it is not OK to persuade someone. They could feel pressured, which means that their behaviour is no longer voluntary. You shouldn't kiss or touch someone if they don't feel comfortable with it.'

When a girl wants to wear a sexy top to school, there might be a problem with the context.

> 'You are about to leave for school wearing a sexy top. What do you think will happen? How will it make others feel and react? It is OK to wear sexy clothes, but school isn't the best place to wear this.'

If someone makes a sexual comment about a classmate, there is no consent, nor is it appropriate for the context.

> 'You are making a sexual comment about a classmate. What message are you giving? What is bothering you? It is OK to think someone is attractive or to have an opinion about how someone looks. It is not OK to make comments about these things in public though. Your classmate hasn't asked you to do that and these kinds of comments can be offensive and make others feel uncomfortable.'

With red flag behaviour the priority is to stop it, but the next steps are no different from yellow flag behaviours. You describe what you have seen, you state which boundaries have been crossed and you discuss what the children should do differently. Because red flag behaviour is more serious, you have to make sure that the adolescents understand the ban and the consequences. Fortunately, red flag behaviour isn't something all young people and adults will have to deal with. It isn't rare, but it's not a part of most young people's development either. We give you two examples of red flag situations and a summary of appropriate responses below. Both examples come directly from Sensoa's Flag System:

> Situation: A 16 year old girl is sleeping in her bed. Her 17 year old brother comes into her bedroom and touches her bottom.

Sexually experimental behaviour sometimes takes place at home between siblings of any age. This can be anything from green to black flag behaviour. So let's take a look at the criteria in this situation.

The girl didn't give her consent as she is sleeping, engagement isn't voluntary because the brother touches her without her knowing and the situation isn't equal because the girl isn't capable of responding because she is asleep. At this age the boy should know that it is inappropriate to touch somebody without their consent. The situation is also of concern because they live in the same house and this could happen every night. This behaviour can be harmful for both parties because the girl may feel anxious/scared/afraid and the boy could get a bad reputation. In addition, their relationship is likely to suffer from his actions.

When one or more of the first three criteria aren't met, a red flag is often assigned. Clearly, this is the case in this situation. The response should focus on the behaviour itself, the fact that she is his sister is not relevant. For example: *'You went into your sister's room without her permission and touched her bottom. How do you think this would make her feel? She was sleeping and couldn't say no. She needs to feel safe in her room, without being afraid of you coming in to watch and touch her. This should never happen again. Are we agreed?'*

It's also important for the parents to supervise to prevent this kind of behaviour reoccurring.

> Situation: Two boys, age 12 and 17, masturbate each other in a changing room at the local swimming pool.

In this situation, the first issue is that there is an age difference of five years between these boys and this is one reason why the situation is assigned a red flag. For teenagers, five years is significant because they will have very different developmental needs. The oldest may have sexual thoughts and may regularly engage in sexual behaviours, but the 12 year old may not be ready for this kind of sexual behaviour. So, for the youngest boy this isn't age appropriate and it might be difficult to be clear about what he wants and doesn't want because he looks up to the older boy; they are not equal. Furthermore, there is a problem with the context; the boys could easily get caught in the changing room. It would be shocking for other people and it might have consequences for the boys in that they may be bullied.

If the same behaviour took place between two 17 year olds, most of the issues outlined above would be irrelevant, but it would still be a yellow flag situation because of the context of the changing room.

The response, therefore, needs to address the age difference (the inequality) and the context. For example: *'I've heard that you masturbated a 12 year old boy. Did he consent to that? Do you think he really felt free to say yes or no with you being so much older than him or did he just join in because he wanted to be friends with you? This kind of behaviour is only OK between people of the same age, even if your young friend initiated it. The age difference between both of you is too big. This could be seen as assault. You also shouldn't do this kind of thing in a public changing room, because you could offend people and there might be consequences for you. This shouldn't happen again. If it does, we will need to take further action. Are we agreed?'*

Of course a conversation with the younger boy is also required and you may choose to involve both boys' parents.

If you have to deal with red flag situations, we recommend that you discuss the situation with professionals and read the full Flag System book.[3]

Black flag behaviour is rarely seen between young children of an approximately equal age and stage of development, but occurs more often with teenagers. Sexual behaviour between adolescents and adults can also be assigned a black flag. Some examples of black flag situations are a 14 year old boy secretly taking pictures of a girl from his class in the shower and posting them online, or a 15 year old girl being held down by two boys while a third one undresses her. Another example is a 23 year old teacher having sexual intercourse with a 15 year old pupil.

It is important to note that black flag behaviour often involves illegal behaviours and it is not something you should deal with on your own. For this reason, we have chosen not to work through examples as this could give the impression that this is straightforward. If you witness a black flag situation, we advise you to seek professional support.

While you've been reading through these different responses, we hope that you've noticed that this process isn't about punishment, but it isn't about being laissez faire either. Your response should contribute to the young person's development. Punishment can lead to teenagers becoming secretive about sexuality, but if you don't intervene at all adolescents won't learn how to deal with unacceptable sexual behaviour in a healthy way. So, being understanding but at the same time very clear is key.

Putting this into action

Let's go back to the exercises at the beginning of this chapter. Consider the four situations again and ask yourself:

- Are all six criteria met?

- If they aren't, to what extent is each criterion not met?

- Which flag do you think best fits the situation?

- How could you respond in each situation?

Drawing on the Flag System's guidance, this is our appraisal of each situation:

Situation 1: Two 13 year old girls in a bedroom, caressing one another between and over their thighs. They are enjoying it.

All criteria are met, this is a green flag situation. Some level of experimental behaviour is normal during puberty (see Chapter 5) but a safe context with mutual consent is important. In this situation, the body language and facial expressions shown in the illustration suggests that this is the case and there doesn't seem to be any coercion. However, if one of the girls was to feel under pressure to do something that she isn't ready for, this would become a yellow flag situation.

If you're certain of both girls' voluntary engagement, you don't need to intervene. If you have any doubts though, it would be good to describe what you saw and explain key rules; for example: *'I saw you were touching each other and you seemed to be enjoying it. It's OK to explore each other's bodies, as long as both of you feel comfortable. If you feel pressured in any way, that's not OK. And if you don't feel comfortable anymore, you should say so and stop.'*

> Situation 2: A father walking in on his 16 year old son and his 17 year old girlfriend, who are naked in bed. They are both enjoying it. There are condoms on the bedside table.

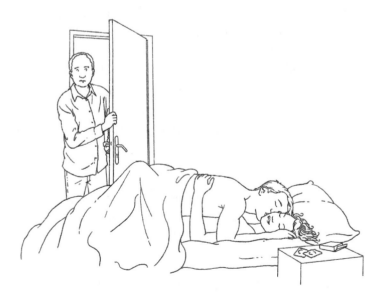

The teenagers' facial expressions suggest mutual consent and their behaviour appears to be voluntary. The teenagers are equal in age and their behaviour is widely perceived as usual at their age. The context of the bedroom is also appropriate. The packet of condoms suggests that they are practising safe sex, so there should be no harmful consequences. This means, in our view, that this is a green flag situation. There is, however, room for discussion regarding the parent entering the room. It's wise to come to an agreement with young people as to how the rest of the family should know when they don't want to be disturbed.

There's no need for any intervention in this situation, and certainly not at that moment! If you want to respond later on, you could perhaps say something positive like: *'I'm sorry I walked in on you earlier. It's lovely that you two are happy together and it's great that you're using condoms. Maybe you can make a "do not disturb" sign, so I don't enter the room when you want some privacy.'*

Before moving on to the next situation, we want to make a note on the 'context' here. Although we as experts, and also as parents, consider this situation to be a green flag, we are aware that some parents wouldn't agree or allow their teenagers of 16 years to have sex in their bedroom or anywhere at all. If the teenagers are aware of this, the colour of the flag shifts to yellow and the parent in this situation has the right to stop the behaviour and explain that this isn't allowed in their house. However, it's impossible to guarantee that the teenagers won't find somewhere else, that is perhaps less safe, to be intimate with each other. Every adolescent has to deal with sexual development and parents and carers can help them by creating a safe context.

> Situation 3: A 15 year old girl having anal sex with her boyfriend. She has consented to it but doesn't like it. She agrees to it because she doesn't want to lose her boyfriend.

The girl has given her consent, but the boy should question

whether her engagement is voluntary and whether the relationship is really equal. This behaviour is uncommon for this age but does happen. In this case the impact could be negative. This situation is, therefore, assigned a red flag, but before we go on to describe an appropriate response, let's take a better look at the criteria.

The girl has given her consent because she doesn't want to lose her boyfriend, but visibly she doesn't like it. So her verbal consent is inconsistent with her non-verbal signals. In this situation consent needs to be re-established and behaviours need to be changed. However, this doesn't happen despite her visible reluctance. Therefore, it is questionable as to whether she is engaging voluntarily. Whether both parties are equal is also doubtful, because the boy determines what sexual act they perform. Although uncommon, anal sex happens at this age. The criterion of impact isn't met because the boy shows harmful behaviour towards the girl. He has put his wishes before hers and if they haven't taken the appropriate precautions she could get physically hurt (see Chapter 7).

If you were told about this situation, you should talk to the teenagers. Your response to both teenagers, separately or together, should emphasize two issues: checking for consent both before and during the act and respecting other people's wishes and boundaries. For example: *You were having anal sex. If you both like it, that would be OK. But I heard that you didn't like it and that it hurt. This can happen with anal sex.* You could then explain a little about anal sex: relaxation, taking time and using a water-based lubricant and appropriate condom. Then continue: *Consent was unclear here – you/she said yes but your/ her body language said no. It's important to know that people can always change their mind after saying "yes". It's perfectly OK to say "yes" at first and "no" later on. Sometimes people don't do this verbally so you should pay attention to other, non-verbal signals. And if there is any doubt about this, you should never be forceful to get your way. Sex is most fun when it's good for both partners. What can we agree on? Do you want to learn more about consent?'*

> Situation 4: Two 16 year olds are having oral sex in the bushes. They both like it.

There is mutual consent and both parties engage voluntarily. In reality, you might be unsure about this, in which case you would need to ask questions to determine what the situation is. Both parties are equal and this behaviour does happen at this age, even though many 16 year olds won't have experienced sexual intercourse or oral sex yet. However, the behaviour isn't OK for the context; others might see them and feel offended or even unsafe. It is also possible that people might take photos or videos of them. In most cases young people choose these kinds of locations because they haven't got anywhere else to go where they can experiment with sexual behaviour in a safe environment. Because of the problems with the context, this situation would be assigned a yellow flag, meaning that you must respond. You might say something like: *'I understand you want to have oral sex with each other, is that right, do you both want to have oral sex with each other? It's OK if you both want this, you are old enough to make this decision. But, this isn't a safe place, because people could easily see you and be offended and there might also be consequences for you if you are seen. So, let's talk about alternatives that are acceptable.'*

You may have been surprised at our application of the criteria in these examples but hopefully our explanations will have helped you understand why we have come to these conclusions and recommendations. To help you put the Flag System into action here are a few more examples:

> Situation: Two 15 year old girls make sexist remarks about the clothes a 17 year old girl is wearing who passes by: *'What a short skirt!' 'Yeah, she looks really slutty.'* The girl can hear what they are saying.

The 17 year old girl didn't give permission to the others to make these comments, so there is no consent. The 15 year old girls weren't forced to say this, so their behaviour was voluntary. The 17 year old girl probably chose her outfit herself, meaning her choice of clothes was voluntary as well. There is no real equality, because although the girls are about the same age, the girls who made the remarks are together, which could make the other girl feel intimidated. Although this kind of behaviour can be expected at this age, the girls are also old enough to know what effect their words could have on others. This behaviour isn't appropriate in any context. It's difficult to know the impact of the situation for the 17 year old girl, she may be upset by the remarks or she may not be bothered.

This is a yellow flag situation. You might say something like this to the two 15 year olds: *'I heard you make sexist remarks about another girl's clothing. How do you think you made her feel? It's OK to have your own style and opinions about how to dress, but it's not OK to criticize someone in public about the way they dress.'*

If the two girls in this scenario were replaced by two boys who made similar comments or a sexist remark to the girl, your comments could be similar. The way someone dresses should never be considered an invitation to make sexist remarks or, indeed, to do anything against their will.

> Situation: Two 13 year old boys are chatting to each other on their smartphones about sex. They are both in their respective bedrooms and are enjoying the conversation.

Using social media and video technology to communicate is very normal for most teenagers. It often makes it easier to talk more freely with each other and these conversations can increase their trust in each other and enhance their self-esteem. The boys probably didn't give their explicit consent for the conversation, but they did interpret each other's response as consensual. They are voluntarily participating and no pressure is being exerted by either of them. In this situation, the boys are equal. Their behaviour is age appropriate in that they are acquiring knowledge about sex with their peers. The context is appropriate since it is taking place in the privacy of their bedrooms and they know each other. There are no harmful consequences; on the contrary, it's likely to have a positive effect.

All the criteria are met and so this is a green flag situation. You don't need to respond, but if you want to, you might say: *'I heard you chatting about sex with each other. Was it good fun? It's OK for you to chat about sex, but make sure that you have these conversations in a safe environment and only with people you know. If you ever want to know anything you can always ask me.'*

Experiences with the Flag System

A common mistake after being introduced to the Flag System is to just use parts of it instead of following all the steps. We see this a lot during training sessions. When we give scenarios to participants, they often assign flags without first using the criteria. As a result, they are guided by their gut instinct rather than objectivity. Frequently we hear *'I think it's a red flag'*, but when we say *'OK, tell us why, which criteria aren't met?,'* the response is often *'Hmmm, I don't know, none actually'*. More often than not, when participants go back and review the scenario against the criteria, the red flag becomes green or yellow.

Even if the steps are followed it's worth noting that dilemmas can still arise. As we mentioned earlier, we have found that people experience difficulties in interpreting the appropriateness of behaviours within different contexts. This is often due to cultural differences, but within any culture there are variations with communities, families and individuals having their own norms. So, what happens if you feel very strongly that the context makes the behaviour unacceptable? Especially if the context is very nuanced and particular? In our workshops, we often need to emphasize that the colour of the flag can shift only by one, because of a problem with the context. According to the Flag System green behaviour can never be red just because you don't like it. Differences in opinion regarding context can lead to discussions between colleagues which is one of the benefits of using the criteria; it encourages everyone to reflect on their personal values when there is a big difference between assigned flags. Discussions about sexual behaviour tend to be much less emotional and more nuanced when using the Flag System.

Another dilemma that has arisen during training workshops is that people can be inclined to change their response out of concern for what other adults, especially parents, might think of them. Examples we use in training workshops include situations like two boys showing each other their erections on a school camp or two 17 year olds having oral sex in the bedroom. Most people initially score these situations green, which is correct, but some of them still feel inclined to stop what's happening, out of concern for what other parents might say if they knew about this behaviour. This isn't necessarily wrong, but it's important to be aware as to why you would stop their behaviour, so that you can explain this to the teenagers, rather than just telling them their actions are wrong.

Experts from Sensoa tell us that most mistakes when applying a flag occur when the situation involves explicit sexual behaviour. The more explicit the behaviour is, the more negatively the behaviour is scored. But sexual experimentation is part of adolescent development, so professionals who work with teenagers should be aware of this, because they are likely to be involuntarily confronted with this behaviour at some point. The tendency to score these situations negatively lies more in one's own resistance than in the harm posed to the teenagers. It is, therefore, a good idea to ask yourself if any objections you have serve yourself or the adolescents.

Another bias that experts have observed is that sexual behaviours that score green in face-to-face contexts often score yellow or red if the behaviour is online. This isn't always appropriate. Of course, young people should be aware of the risks involved in sharing information online, but when there are clear agreements it is not so different from traditional face-to-face contexts.

A real strength of the Flag System that people have reported to us is that the criteria can be applied to other aspects of children's and teenagers' social development. For example, criteria like mutual consent or equality are relevant to other non-sexual behaviours. Applying this approach to everyday life can normalize relationships and sexuality education because the 'rules' are consistent across all aspects of development. For example, when siblings 'borrow' each other's clothes without asking or when pressure is put on a teenager to steal something or to smoke a cigarette, the same principles apply. When we realize this, relationships and sexuality education stops being quite so different and separate from other aspects of rearing children and teenagers.

An additional strength of the Flag System is that in addition to being of value to professionals, carers and parents, it can be useful for young people too. Teenagers who have learned about and practised using the Flag System often say that their perceptions match the explanation and that they find it helpful to have the language to enable them to explain their judgements. Discussing 'consent' with teenagers and asking them to formulate their own criteria could be an effective exercise in which parents, carers and teachers could introduce the six criteria of the Flag System.

Finally, the Flag System also helps to open up discussions which challenge the taboo of discussing sexual assault. This is very valuable because victims can only get help if they are able to talk about what happened. In addition, by giving victims a voice, the power is taken away from the perpetrator as the silence that has historically surrounded sexual assault, and has allowed the perpetrator to hide, is replaced by open discussion.

Summary

Using the Flag System correctly isn't easy because of the nature of the subject, but even a brief introduction like this can help adults rethink relationships and sexuality education. If you are keen to start using the system, particularly in a professional context, we recommend that you take a look at www.flagsystem. org or obtain the Sensoa Flag System book.[4]

The key messages given in this chapter were:

- The Flag System was initially developed for professionals, but we have found it can also be helpful for non-professionals like parents and carers and even for adolescents themselves.

- The aim of the Flag System is to enable professionals to assess the sexual behaviour of children and adolescents aged 0–18 years by using six types of criteria. These criteria are based on research about developing judgement in a more objective way, and try to enable users to suspend their instinctive reactions which may cloud objectivity.

- The six criteria are the following:

  - mutual consent

  - voluntary engagement

  - equality (in terms of age, knowledge etc.)

  - appropriate for the stage of development (this requires knowledge about the sexual development of children and adolescents)

  - appropriate within the context

- the physical, psychological, emotional and social impact of the specific behaviour on the child or adolescent.

- The specific behaviours get a flag (green, yellow, red or black) based on the level of (un)acceptability of the behaviour, making use of the six criteria.

- When judging the (un)acceptability of a situation, the Flag System focuses on how harmful the situation is for the participants.

- In the chapter several examples are given to illustrate the use of the criteria and the response to the specific behaviours.

Chapter 10

Moving forward

You've reached the end of our book. For some of you, a lot of the information will have been familiar, and for others, less so. Either way, there is a lot to reflect on in how, when and what you will choose to use from all of the discussions presented throughout the previous chapters.

You may remember that back in Chapter 1, we asked you to answer a set of questions. To see what you have taken from this book, we suggest that you repeat the exercise by completing the questions below:

1. Do you know the name of your teenager's best friend?

   a. Yes, it's...
   b. I know my child has friends, but I don't know their names
   c. I don't know

2. Has your teenager has ever experienced bullying (either being bullied or bullying others)?

   a. Yes, I know for sure they have/haven't
   b. I think they have/haven't, but I'm not sure
   c. I really don't know

3. Has your teenager ever drunk alcohol?

   a. Yes, I know for sure they have/haven't
   b. I think they have/haven't, but I'm not certain
   c. I really don't know

4. Has your teenager ever smoked cigarettes?

   a. Yes, I know for sure they have/haven't
   b. I think they have/haven't, but I'm not certain
   c. I really don't know

5. Has your teenager ever tried drugs?

   a. Yes, I know for sure they have/haven't
   b. I think they have/haven't, but I'm not certain
   c. I really don't know

6. Is your child usually happy?

   a. Yes, I'm sure they are/aren't
   b. I think they are/aren't, but I'm not sure
   c. I really don't know

7. Has your child ever been in love?

   a. I know for sure they have/haven't
   b. I think they have/haven't, but I'm not sure
   c. I really don't know

8. Does your child masturbate?

   a. I know for sure they do/don't
   b. I think they do/don't, but I'm not sure
   c. I really don't know

9. Do you know whether your teenager has ever watched porn?

   a. I know for sure they have/haven't
   b. I think they have/haven't but I'm not sure
   c. I really don't know

10. Has your child ever engaged in sexual behaviour with someone else?

    a. I know for sure they have/haven't
    b. I think they have/haven't, but I'm not sure
    c. I really don't know

11. Has your child ever had negative experiences with sexuality?

    a. I know for sure they have/haven't
    b. I think they have/haven't, but I'm not sure
    c. I really don't know

Now compare your responses with those you gave when you started to read our book. Are there any differences in your answers? Has anything changed in your thinking?

We hope that you have noticed some positive changes when comparing your responses with those you gave in Chapter 1. We also hope that you are able to identify some changes in your perceptions of adolescents and young people's sexual development and, perhaps, a greater awareness of your own ideas, personal values and opinions regarding relationships and sexuality. And, ultimately, we hope that all of this thinking and reflection will positively impact upon how you convey messages regarding relationships and sexuality education. Because this was our aim in writing this book.

Although relationships and sexuality education should be underpinned by evidence-based facts, we realize that personal values play a significant role in what messages are delivered and how they are conveyed. Throughout adolescence, young people will form their own opinions and values. They will do this by listening and using everything that they hear and observe from the peer group they want to belong to, as well as from teachers, books, media and, of course, social media. For parents and carers, it can sometimes feel like we become redundant as adolescents progress through the teenage years (apart from the laundry, cooking and cleaning!), but don't underestimate your influence. You planted a seed, long ago, the day you met your child. That seed has grown up and is flourishing now, ready to be enjoyed by others. But as with plants, flowers and all living creatures, when they are ready to flourish, they still need care, attention and support. So does your teenager. And sometimes even after they are 18 years old!

Parents and carers remain parents and carers for many years! Despite their need for independence, adolescents and young adults still need the warmth, love and support of the special adults in their lives. When you see 18 year olds at work or at university they may seem fully mature, but many still long to be hugged, cared for and helped with making important decisions. The same applies to many young people beyond 18 too. Although the law in many countries might say an 18 year old is an adult and is allowed to drink alcohol, vote, marry and would be considered an adult in a court of law, the lived realities of many young people who have reached this age are quite different. Many of them haven't yet had a sexual relationship, most don't want to marry and some don't want to drink alcohol. They may still live at home with their parents, and may be struggling with relationships, sexual feelings and falling in love. The list goes on, but in short, to become 'a real adult' more autonomy is needed than the level of autonomy many 18 year olds have reached.

The road towards autonomy is not always an easy one. And for some it can be a never-ending journey to reach real autonomy, even in adulthood. Although your 18 year old will step into the big wide world and will be treated (and feel) like an adult, you will always be their parent or carer. The process of letting your teenager go is a long one and sometimes a difficult one. Letting go doesn't mean taking your hands off and throwing them into deep water. Letting go means standing by from a distance and watching them step or jump into the water in their own way. Letting go means still being available when the young adult needs answers or support. Letting go also means that a parent or carer doesn't need to know everything about the young person anymore, because to become an adult, they need privacy and they need the freedom to make mistakes and learn from them. So, letting go means having faith in your child and trusting them to make their own decisions and to ask for your support whenever that is needed.

This brings us back to the key message that we have tried to convey throughout our book: a central goal of relationships and sexuality education is to enable young people to reach sexual well-being and to be happy and confident with their sexuality. Not by demanding that they achieve this but by helping them find their own way and by supporting them to take care of themselves. As parents, carers and educators we can feel satisfied with all our efforts when we see our teenagers develop through to the end of adolescence to find happiness and well-being in their self-chosen network of friends, lovers and partners. That is when we can sit back, relax and tell ourselves: 'We have done a good job.'

We sincerely hope that our book has made some small contribution to you reaching that moment! Cherish your young people and enjoy this journey together.

Sanderijn, Clare and Arris

Resources

General

Atalanta, H. (2019) *A Celebration of Vulva Diversity*. www.thisisusbooks.com. See also www.thevulvagallery.com

Brochmann, N. and Støkken Dahl, E. (2018) *The Wonder Down Under: A User's Guide to the Vagina*. London: Yellow Kite.

Chavez Perez, I. (2020) *Respect: Everything a Guy Needs to Know About Sex, Love and Consent*. London: Piatkus.

Frans, E. (2018) *Sensoa Flag System, Reacting to Sexually (Un)Acceptable Behaviour of Children and Young People*. Antwerpen/Apeldoorn: Sensoa/Garant.

Haffner, D. (2004) *From Diapers to Dating*. New York: Newmarket Press.

Orenstein, P. (2016) *Boys & Sex*. New York: HarperCollins.

Orenstein, P. (2020) *Girls & Sex*. London: Souvenir Press.

Rough, B.J. (2018) *Beyond Birds & Bees*. New York: Seal Press.

Resources about diversity

Barker, M.-J. and Scheele, J. (2016) *Queer*. London: Icon Books.

Dawson, J. (2021) *This Book is Gay* (2nd revised edn). Naperville, IL: Sourcebooks Fire.

Hardell, A. (2016) *The ABC's of LGBT+*. Miami, FL: Mango Media.

Hoffman-Fox, D. (2017) *You and Your Gender Identity*. New York: Skyhorse Publishing.

Owens-Reid, D. and Russo, K. (2014) *This Is a Book for Parents of Gay Kids*. San Francisco, CA: Chronicle Books.

The Genderbread Person – a teaching tool for breaking the big concept of gender down into bite-sized, digestible pieces. www.genderbread.org

Australia

Australian Institute of Health and Welfare – links and other information about child protection in all states and territories. www.aihw.gov.au/reports-data/health-welfare-services/child-protection/links-other-information

eSafety – online safety information. Includes anonymous reporting of offensive and illegal content. www.esafety.gov.au

HealthyWA – information on parenting, immunizations, sexual health, safety and first aid, treatments and health care options. www.healthywa.wa.gov.au. See below the link for *Talk Soon, Talk Often* from HealthyWA.

Kids Helpline – free confidential 24/7 phone and online counselling service for 5–25 year olds in Australia. 1800 55 1800 or www.kidshelpline.com.au

Parenting WA Line – 24-hour phone service: information, support and referral service for parents, carers and families with children up to 18 years. (08) 6279 1200 or 1800 654 432.

Q-life – phone and online counselling for LGBTIQ+ people and their family and friends (all ages). 1800 184 527 or https://qlife.org.au

Raising Children Network – the scientifically validated content is translated into everyday language to help parents and carers make decisions that work for them in their individual family circumstances. https://raisingchildren.net.au/teens

ReachOut – ReachOut is the most accessed mental health service for young people in Australia. https://au.reachout.com/relationships/sex

ReachOut Parents – ReachOut Parents provides information, tools and resources to help parents and carers support 12–18 year olds in their family environment. https://parents.au.reachout.com/common-concerns/everyday-issues/things-to-try-talking-about-sex

Sex Ed Rescue – a resource for parents. https://sexedrescue.com

Strong Families Safe Kids – advice and referral line in Tasmania. www.strongfamiliessafekids.tas.gov.au

Talk Soon, Talk Often: A Guide for Parents Talking to Their Kids about Sex. www.healthywa.wa.gov.au/~/media/HWA/Documents/Healthy-living/Sexual-health/talk-soon-talk-often.pdf

Canada

The Access Line – confidential 24-hour Canada-wide toll-free number that provides information on reproductive and sexual health. 1 888 642 2725.

Action Canada for Sexual Health & Rights – a progressive, pro-choice charitable organization committed to advancing and upholding sexual and reproductive health and rights in Canada and globally. www.actioncanadashr.org

Kids Help Phone – phone for help for abuse, bullying, cyberbullying, harassment, relationship violence and sexual exploitation or whatever a child wants to talk about. Offers professional counselling, information and referrals for young people in both English and French. 1 800 668 6868 or https://kidshelpphone.ca

Sex Information & Education Council of Canada (SIECCAN) (2019) *Canadian Guidelines for Sexual Health Education* – a guide for educators and policy makers regarding comprehensive sexuality education in Canada. https://siecus.org/wp-content/uploads/2020/03/NSES-2020-2.pdf. SIECCAN is a not-for-profit charitable organization that works with health professionals, educators, community organizations, governments and corporate partners to promote sexual and reproductive health.

SHORE Centre – offers inclusive sexual and reproductive health services that uphold the dignity of everyone. www.shorecentre.ca

UK

BISH (best in sexual health) – sex and relationships advice for over 14s. For anyone thinking about sex, how you feel about you, and your relationships. Developed by Justin Hancock in 2009. www.bishuk.com

Brook – operates a number of sexual health and well-being services across the UK and is committed to supporting young people. www.brook.org.uk

Lucy Faithfull Foundation – offers a range of services for individuals and families looking for help, advice, support and intervention with issues relating to child sexual abuse. www.lucyfaithfull.org.uk

Mermaids – helps gender-diverse kids, young people and their families. www.mermaidsuk.org.uk

NSPCC (National Society for the Prevention of Cruelty to Children) – support, advice and information concerning all aspects of children's well-being. www.nspcc.org.uk

Outspoken Sex Ed – a social enterprise which promotes open parent-child sexuality communication. www.outspokeneducation.com

Stonewall – stands for lesbian, gay, bi, trans, queer, questioning and ace (LGBTQ+) people everywhere. They imagine a world where all LGBTQ+ people are free to be themselves and we can live our lives to the full. www.stonewall.org.uk

USA

Advocates for Youth – focuses on adolescent reproductive and sexual health, strengthening the ability of youth to make informed, responsible decisions about their sexual health. There is also a page for parents on the website as well as a video series to help parents talk to kids from as young as 4 years old to 14 about where babies come from and growing up. https://advocatesforyouth.org

Answer – national organization that provides and promotes unfettered access to comprehensive sexuality education for young people and the adults who teach them. https://answer.rutgers.edu

Child Welfare Information Gateway – promotes the safety, permanency and well-being of children, youth and families by connecting child welfare, adoption and related professionals as well as the public to information, resources and tools covering topics on child welfare, child abuse and neglect, out-of-home care, adoption and more. www.childwelfare.gov

Committee for Children – provides tools to promote the safety, well-being and success of children in school and in life. www.cfchildren.org

Lesbian, Gay, Bisexual and Transgender Concerns Office – aims to advance psychology as a means of improving the health and well-being of lesbian, gay, bisexual and transgender people, increasing understanding of gender identity and sexual orientation as aspects of human diversity, and reducing stigma, prejudice, discrimination and violence toward LGBT people. www.apa.org/pi/lgbt

National Center on the Sexual Behavior of Youth (NCSBY) – provides national training and technical assistance to improve the accuracy, accessibility and strategic use of accurate information about the nature, incidence, prevalence, prevention, treatment and management of youth with problematic sexual behaviour. www.ncsby.org

National Sex Education Standards (2nd edn) – outlines the foundational knowledge and skills students need to navigate sexual development and grow into sexually healthy adults. https://advocatesforyouth.org/wp-content/uploads/2020/03/NSES-2020-web.pdf

Netsmartz – provides information on internet safety including sexting, social media, gaming, cyberbullying and so on. www.missingkids.org/NetSmartz

Planned Parenthood – delivers information and materials on reproductive health care and sex education to millions of people worldwide, and for parents. www.plannedparenthood.org

Sexuality Information and Education Council of the United States (SIECUS) – asserts that sex education is a powerful vehicle for social change. It views sexuality as a fundamental part of being human, one worthy of dignity and respect. It advocates for the rights of all people to accurate information, comprehensive sexuality education and the full spectrum of sexual and reproductive health services. https://siecus.org

Sexuality Resource Center for Parents – helps parents provide positive comprehensive sexuality education, raising sexually healthy and happy children. www.srcp.org/index.html

Stop It Now! – prevents the sexual abuse of children by mobilizing adults, families and communities to take actions that protect children before they are harmed. www.stopitnow.org

The Playbook – a place where teens can find accurate information about sexual health and birth control. www.teenplaybook.org/#

Endnotes

Introduction

1   Kågesten, A., Page, A. and van Reeuwijk, M. (2019) *A Conceptual Framework for Adolescent Sexual Wellbeing*. Mexico City: World Association for Sexual Health Congress.

2   WHO (2021) *Adolescent Health*. Accessed on 18/09/2021 at www.who. int/health-topics/adolescent-health#tab=tab_1

Chapter 1

1   Schwarz, B., Mayer, B., Trommsdorff, G., Ben-Arieh, A., Friedlmeier, M., Lubiewska, K., Mishra, R. and Peltzer, K. (2012) 'Does the importance of parent and peer relationships for adolescents' life satisfaction vary across cultures?' *Journal of Early Adolescence 32*, 55–80.

2   Ma, C.Q. and Huebner, E.S. (2008) 'Attachment relationships and adolescents' life satisfaction: Some relationships matter more to girls than boys'. *Psychology in the Schools 45*, 177–190.

3   Suldo, S. and Fefer, S. (2015) 'Parent-Child Relationships and Well-Being'. In C.L. Proctor and P.A. Linley (eds) *Research, Applications, and Interventions for Children and Adolescents: A Positive Psychology Perspective*. New York: Springer.

4   Krauss, S., Orth, U. and Robins, R.W. (2020) 'Family environment and self-esteem development: A longitudinal study from age 10 to 16'. *Journal of Personality and Social Psychology 119*, 2, 457–478.

5   Nogueira Avelar e Silva, R., van de Bongardt, D., van de Looij-Jansen, P., Wijtzes, A. and Raat, H. (2016) 'Mother – and father – adolescent

relationships and early sexual intercourse'. *Pediatrics*, e20160782. DOI: 10.1542/peds.2016-0782.

6 Anderson, J.R. (2020) 'Inviting autonomy back to the table: The importance of autonomy for healthy relationship functioning'. *Journal of Marital and Family Therapy 46*, 1, 3–14.

7 Steinberg, L. (1999) *Adolescence* (5th edn). Boston, MA: McGraw-Hill.

8 Gottman, J. and Declaire, J. (1997) *The Heart of Parenting: How to Raise an Emotionally Intelligent Child*. New York: Simon & Schuster.

9 ibid.

10 Kyriazos, T.A. and Stalikas, A. (2018) 'Positive parenting or positive psychology parenting? Towards a conceptual framework of positive psychology parenting'. *Psychology 9*, 7, 1761–1788.

Seligman, M. (2002) *Authentic Happiness: Using the New Positive Psychology to Realize your Potential for Lasting Fulfilment*. New York: Free Press.

See also the Triple P website for principles of the Positive Parenting Program: www.triplep.net/glo-en/home

11 Baumrind, D. (1991) 'Parenting Styles and Adolescent Development'. In J. Brooks-Gunn, R.M. Lerner and A.C. Petersen (eds) *The Encyclopedia on Adolescence*. New York: Garland Publishing.

12 ibid.

13 Ma and Huebner, 'Attachment relationships and adolescents' life satisfaction'.

14 Ream, G.L. and Savin-Williams, R.C. (2005) 'Reciprocal associations between adolescent sexual activity and quality of youth-parent interactions'. *Journal of Family Psychology 19*, 2, 171–179.

15 Moore, K.A., Guzman, L., Hair, E., Lippman, L. and Garrett, S. (2004) 'Parent-teen relationships and interactions: Far more positive than not'. *Child Trends 25*, 1–8.

Dittus, P.J., Michael, S.L., Becasen, J.S., Gloppen, K.M., McCarthy, K. and Guilamo-Ramos, V. (2015) 'Parental monitoring and its associations with adolescent sexual risk behavior: A meta-analysis'. *Pediatrics 136*, 6, e1587–e1599.

16 Lind, J., Ghirlanda, S. and Enquist, M. (2019) 'Social learning through associative processes: A computational theory'. *Royal Society Open Science 6*. DOI: https://doi.org/10.1098/rsos.181777.

17 Dittus *et al.*, 'Parental monitoring and its associations with adolescent sexual risk behavior'.

18 UNICEF UK (2013) *The Well-Being of Children: Short Version of the Report for Young People in the UK*. Accessed on 18/09/2021 at www.unicef.org.uk/publications/report-card-11-child-wellbeing-what-do-you-think

UNICEF (2020) *Innocenti Report Card 16. Worlds of Influence: Understanding What Shapes Child Well-Being in Rich Countries.* Accessed on 18/09/2021 at www.Report-Card-16-Worlds-of-Influence-child-wellbeing.pdf (unicef-irc.org)

19 Boztas, S. (2018) 'Why Dutch Teenagers are among the Happiest in the World'. *The Guardian*, 17 June. Accessed on 18/09/2021 at www.theguardian.com/world/2018/jun/17/why-dutch-bring-up-worlds-happiest-teenagers

20 WHO (2020) *Spotlight on Adolescent Health and Well-Being. Findings from the 2017/2018 Health Behaviour in School-aged Children (HBSC) Survey in Europe and Canada.* Accessed on 18/09/2021 at www.euro.who.int/en/publications/abstracts/spotlight-on-adolescent-health-and-well-being.-findings-from-the-20172018-health-behaviour-in-school-aged-children-hbsc-survey-in-europe-and-canada.-international-report.-volume-1.-key-findings

21 ibid.

22 Smit, K., Voogt, C., Hiemstra, M., Kleinjan, M., Otten, R. and Kuntsche, E. (2018) 'Development of alcohol expectancies and early alcohol use in children and adolescents: A systematic review'. *Clinical Psychology Review* 60, 136–146.

23 WHO, *Spotlight on Adolescent Health and Well-Being.*

24 SAMHSA (2021) *National Survey on Drug Use and Health.* Accessed on 18/09/2021 at www.samhsa.gov/data/data-we-collect/nsduh-national-survey-drug-use-and-health

25 WHO, *Spotlight on Adolescent Health and Well-Being.*

26 NHS Digital (2019) *Smoking, Drinking and Drug Use among Young People in England 2018.* Accessed on 18/09/2021 at https://digital.nhs.uk/data-and-information/publications/statistical/smoking-drinking-and-drug-use-among-young-people-in-england/2018

27 SAMHSA, *National Survey on Drug Use and Health.*

28 WHO, *Spotlight on Adolescent Health and Well-Being.*

29 ibid.

30 SAMHSA, *National Survey on Drug Use and Health.*

31 Australian Institute of Health and Welfare (2020) *National Drug Strategy Household Survey 2019.* Accessed on 18/09/2021 at www.aihw.gov.au/reports/illicit-use-of-drugs/national-drug-strategy-household-survey-2019/contents/summary

32 Martellozzo, E., Monaghan, A., Davidson, J. and Adler, J. (2020) 'Researching the effects that online pornography has on UK adolescents aged 11 to 16'. *SAGE Open.* DOI: 10.1177/2158244019899462.

33 Barna Group (2016) *Teens & Young Adults Use Porn More Than Anyone Else.* Accessed on 18/09/2021 at www.barna.com/research/ teens-young-adults-use-porn-more-than-anyone-else

34 Quadara, A., El-Murr, A. and Latham, J. (2017) *The Effects of Pornography on Children and Young People.* Accessed on 18/09/2021 at https://aifs.gov.au/publications/ effects-pornography-children-and-young-people-snapshot

35 De Graaf, H., Van den Borne, M., Nikkelen, S., Twisk, D. and Meijer, S. (2017) *Seks onder je 25e (Sex Under the Age of 25).* Utrecht: Rutgers/ Soa Aids, Eburon.

36 Dalenberg, W.G., Timmermans, M.C. and Van Geert, P.L.C. (2018) 'Dutch adolescents' everyday expressions of sexual behavior trajectories over a 2-year period: A mixed-methods study'. *Archives of Sexual Behavior 47*, 6, 1811–1823.

37 Act for Youth (2020) *Youth Statistics: Sexual Health.* Accessed on 18/09/2021 at https://actforyouth.net/adolescence/demographics/ sexual_health.cfm

38 The Australian Institute of Family Studies (2019) *Growing up in Australia: The Longitudinal Study of Australian Children (LSAC) Annual Statistical Report 2018.* Accessed on 18/09/2021 at https://growingupinaustralia. gov.au/research-findings/annual-statistical-reports-2018

39 De Graaf *et al., Seks onder je 25e.*

40 Fisher, C.M., Waling, A., Kerr, L., Bellamy, R., Ezer, P., Mikolajczak, G., Brown, G., Carman, M. and Lucke, J. (2019) *6th National Survey of Australian Secondary Students and Sexual Health 2018.* Melbourne: La Trobe. DOI: http://dx.doi.org/10.26181/5c80777f6c35e.

41 Kaestle, C.E. and Allen, K.R. (2011) 'The role of masturbation in healthy sexual development: Perceptions of young adults'. *Archives of Sexual Behavior 40*, 983–994. DOI: https://doi.org/10.1007/ s10508-010-9722-0.

42 WHO, *Spotlight on Adolescent Health and Well-Being.*

43 Lenhart, A., Anderson, M. and Smith, A. (2015) *Teens, Technology and Romantic Relationships.* Accessed on 18/09/2021 at www.pewresearch. org/internet/2015/10/01/basics-of-teen-romantic-relationships

44 Lewis, R., Tanton, C., Mercer, C.H., Mitchell, K.R., Palmer, M., Macdowall, W. and Wellings, K. (2017) 'Heterosexual practices among young people in Britain: Evidence from three national surveys of sexual attitudes and lifestyles'. *Journal of Adolescent Health 61*, 6, 694–702.

Chapter 2

1   WHO (2015) *Brief Sexuality-Related Communication: Recommendations for a Public Health Approach.* Accessed on 18/09/2021 at www.who.int/reproductivehealth/publications/sexual_health/sexuality-related-communication/en

2   International Planned Parenthood Federation (IPPF) (2010) *IPPF Framework for Comprehensive Sexuality Education.* London: IPPF.

3   UNFPA (2015) *Emerging Evidence, Lessons and Practice in Comprehensive Sexuality Education: A Global Review.* Accessed on 18/09/2021 at www.unfpa.org/publications/emerging-evidence-lessons-and-practice-comprehensive-sexuality-education-global-review

4   Kågesten, A. and Van Reeuwijk, M. (2021) 'Adolescent sexual wellbeing: A conceptual framework'. *SocArXiv.* DOI: http://dx.doi.org/10.31235/osf.io/9as6e.

5   Harris, J.R. (1998) *The Nurture Assumption: Why Children Turn Out the Way They Do.* New York: The Free Press.

6   De Haas, B. and Hutter, I. (2021) 'Teachers' personal experiences of sexual initiation motivating their sexuality education messages in secondary schools in Kampala, Uganda'. *Sex Education.* DOI: 10.1080/14681811.2021.1898360.

7   Pound, P., Denford, S., Shucksmith, J., Tanton, C. *et al.* (2017) 'What is best practice in sex and relationship education? A synthesis of evidence, including stakeholders' views'. *BMJ Open 7,* 5, e014791.

    Montgomery, P. and Knerr, W. (2018) *Review of the Evidence on Sexuality Education: Report to Inform the Update of the UNESCO International Technical Guidance on Sexuality Education.* Paris: UNESCO.

8   Common Sense Media (2019) *Media Use by Tweens and Teens 2019.* Accessed on 18/09/2021 at www.commonsensemedia.org/Media-use-by-tweens-and-teens-2019-infographic

    Morgan, R. (2016) *9 in 10 Aussie Teens Now Have a Mobile (and Most Are Already on to Their Second or Subsequent Handset).* Accessed on 18/09/2021 at www.roymorgan.com/findings/6929-australian-teenagers-and-their-mobile-phones-june-2016-201608220922

    Statista (2020) *Share of Children Owning Tablets and Smartphones in the United Kingdom (UK) from 2019, by Age.* Accessed on 18/09/2021 at www.statista.com/statistics/805397/children-ownership-of-tablets-smartphones-by-age-uk

9   APA Task Force on the Sexualization of Girls (2008) *Report of the APA Task Force on the Sexualization of Girls.* American Psychological Association. Accessed on 18/09/2021 at www.apa.org/pi/women/programs/girls/report

10 UNESCO (2020) *Switched On: Sexuality Education in the Digital Space*. Accessed on 18/09/2021 at https://healtheducationresources.unesco. org/library/documents/switched-sexuality-education-digital-space

11 ibid.

12 Barrense-Dias, Y., Berchtold, A., Suris, J. and Akre, C. (2017) 'Sexting and the definition issue'. *Journal of Adolescent Health 61*, 5, 544–554.

Chapter 3

1   Lerner, R.M. and Steinberg, L. (eds) (2009) *Handbook of Adolescent Psychology* (3rd edn). Hoboken, NJ: John Wiley & Sons.

Jackson, S. and Goossens, L. (eds) (2006) *Handbook of Adolescent Development* (1st edn). Hove: Psychology Press.

2   De Haas, B. and Hutter, I. (2021) 'Teachers' personal experiences of sexual initiation motivating their sexuality education messages in secondary schools in Kampala, Uganda'. *Sex Education*. DOI: 10.1080/14681811.2021.1898360.

3   Schalet, A.T. (2011) *Not Under My Roof: Parents, Teens and the Culture of Sex*. Chicago, IL, and London: The University of Chicago Press.

4   Hilton, G.L.S. (2003) 'Listening to the boys: English boys' views on the desirable characteristics of teachers of sex education'. *Sex Education 3*, 1, 33–45.

Chapter 4

1   Diamond, A. (2013) 'Executive functions'. *Annual Review of Psychology 64*, 135–168.

2   ibid.

3   ibid.

4   ibid.

Chapter 5

1   De Graaf, H., Van den Borne, M., Nikkelen, S., Twisk, D. and Meijer, S. (2017) *Seks onder je 25e (Sex Under the Age of 25)*. Utrecht: Rutgers/ Soa Aids, Eburon.

2 Jolles, J. (2017) *Het tienerbrein, over de adolescent tussen biologie en omgeving (The Teenage Brain, about the Adolescent between Biology and Environment)*. Amsterdam: Amsterdam University Press.

3 De Graaf *et al.*, *Seks onder je 25e*.

4 Broster, A. (2020) *What is the Orgasm Gap?* Accessed on 18/09/2021 at www.forbes.com/sites/alicebroster/2020/07/31/what-is-the-orgasm-gap/?sh=658ec3c960f8

5 ibid.

6 De Graaf *et al.*, *Seks onder je 25e*.

7 Van der Doef, S. and Reinders, J. (2018) 'Stepwise sexual development of adolescents: The Dutch approach to sexuality education'. *Nature Reviews Urology 15*. DOI: 10.1038/nrurol.2018.3.

8 De Graaf *et al.*, *Seks onder je 25e*.
   Van der Doef and Reinders, 'Stepwise sexual development of adolescents'.

9 De Graaf *et al.*, *Seks onder je 25e*.
   Ethier, K.A., Kann, L. and McManus, T. (2018) 'Sexual intercourse among high school students: 29 states and United States overall, 2005–2015'. *MMWR 66*, 1393–1397.

10 Witwer, E., Jones, R.K. and Lindberg, L.D. (2018) *Sexual Behavior and Contraceptive and Condom Use Among US High School Students, 2013–2017*. New York: Guttmacher Institute. Accessed on 18/09/2021 at www.guttmacher.org/report/sexual-behavior-contraceptive-condom-use-us-high-school-students-2013-2017

11 Julian, K. (2018) 'Why are young people having so little sex?' *The Atlantic*. December. Accessed on 18/09/2021 at www.theatlantic.com/magazine/archive/2018/12/the-sex-recession/573949

12 Cense, M. (2019) 'Navigating a bumpy road: Developing sexuality education that supports young people's sexual agency'. *Sex Education 19*, 3, 263–276.
   TENGA (2020) *TENGA 2020 Self-Pleasure Report*. Accessed on 18/09/2021 at www.tenga.co/press/TENGA_2020_US_Report.pdf

13 De Graaf *et al.*, *Seks onder je 25e*.

14 TENGA, *TENGA 2020 Self-Pleasure Report*.
   Orenstein, P. (2016) *Girls & Sex, Navigating the Complicated New Landscape*. New York: Harper.

15 Lunsen, R. and Laan, E. (2017) *Seks!* Amsterdam: Prometheus.

16 Institute of Medicine (US) Committee on Lesbian, Gay, Bisexual, and Transgender Health Issues and Research Gaps and Opportunities (2011) *The Health of Lesbian, Gay, Bisexual, and Transgender People: Building a Foundation for Better Understanding*. Washington, DC: National Academies Press (US).

17 Ganna, A., Verweij, K.J.H., Nivard, M.G., Maier, R. *et al.* (2019) 'Large-scale GWAS reveals insights into the genetic architecture of same-sex sexual behavior'. *Science 365*, 6456. DOI: 10.1126/science.aat7693.

18 ibid.

19 ibid.

20 Gartrell, N., Bos, H. and Koh, A. (2019) 'Sexual attraction, sexual identity, and same sex sexual experiences of adult offspring in the US National Longitudinal Lesbian Family Study'. *Archives of Sexual Behavior 48*. DOI: 10.1007/s10508-019-1434-5.

21 American Psychological Association, Task Force on Appropriate Therapeutic Responses to Sexual Orientation (2009) *Report of the American Psychological Association Task Force on Appropriate Therapeutic Responses to Sexual Orientation.* Accessed on 18/09/2021 at www.apa.org/pi/lgbt/resources/therapeutic-response.pdf

22 De Graaf *et al.*, *Seks onder je 25e.*

23 ibid.

24 Boydell, V., Wright, K.Q. and Smith, R.D. (2021) 'A rapid review of sexual pleasure in first sexual experience(s)'. *The Journal of Sex Research.* DOI: https://doi.org/10.1080/00224499.2021.1904810.

25 De Graaf *et al.*, *Seks onder je 25e.*

26 ibid.

27 Boydell *et al.*, 'A rapid review of sexual pleasure in first sexual experience(s)'.

28 Loeber, O. (2014) 'Wrestling with the hymen: Consultations and practical solutions'. *The European Journal of Contraception and Reproductive Health Care 20*. DOI: 10.3109/13625187.2014.984834.

29 Jolly, S., Oosterhoff, P., Faith, B., Braeken, D. and Shephard, K. (2020) 'Sexuality education for young people in digital spaces'. Paper commissioned for Switched On: Sexuality Education in the Digital Space, Istanbul, Turkey, 19–22 February.

Chapter 6

1 WHO Regional Office for Europe and BZgA (2010) *Standards for Sexuality Education in Europe.* BZgA Cologne: Federal Centre for Health Education. Accessed on 18/09/2021 at www.bzga-whocc.de/fileadmin/user_upload/WHO_BZgA_Standards_English.pdf

2 UNESCO (2018) *International Technical Guidance on Sexuality Education: An Evidence-Informed Approach.* Paris: UNESCO. Accessed on 18/09/2021 at https://unesdoc.unesco.org/ark:/48223/pf0000260770

3   Sexuality Information and Education Council of the United States (2004) *National Guidelines for Comprehensive Sexuality Education* (3rd edn). New York: SIECUS. Accessed on 18/09/2021 at https://siecus.org/resources/the-guidelines

4   Plan International (2020) *Putting the C in CSE: Standards for Content, Delivery and Environments of Comprehensive Sexuality Education.* Accessed on 18/09/2021 at https://plan-international.org/publications/comprehensive-sexuality-education-standards

5   Western Australian (WA) Department of Health (2019) *Talk Soon, Talk Often: A Guide for Parents Talking to Their Kids about Sex.* State of Western Australia: Department of Health. Accessed on 18/09/2021 at www.healthywa.wa.gov.au/Articles/S_T/Talk-soon-talk-often

6   WHO (2020) *Spotlight on Adolescent Health and Well-Being: Findings from the 2017/2018 Health Behaviour in School-aged Children (HBSC) Survey in Europe and Canada.* Accessed on 18/09/2021 at www.euro.who.int/en/publications/abstracts/spotlight-on-adolescent-health-and-well-being.-findings-from-the-20172018-health-behaviour-in-school-aged-children-hbsc-survey-in-europe-and-canada.-international-report.-volume-1.-key-findings

7   ibid.

8   Jolly, S., Oosterhoff, P., Faith, B., Braeken, D. and Shephard, K. (2020) 'Sexuality education for young people in digital spaces'. Paper commissioned for Switched On: Sexuality Education in the Digital Space, Istanbul, Turkey, 19–22 February.

9   De Graaf, H., Van den Borne, M., Nikkelen, S., Twisk, D. and Meijer, S. (2017) *Seks onder je 25e (Sex Under the Age of 25).* Utrecht: Rutgers/Soa Aids, Eburon.

10 CDC (n.d.) *CDC Fact Sheet: Information for Teens and Young Adults: Staying Healthy and Preventing STDs US.* Accessed on 18/09/2021 at www.cdc.gov/std/life-stages-populations/stdfact-teens.htm

11 Chollier, M., Tomkinson, C. and Philibert, P. (2016) 'STIs/HIV stigma and health: A short review'. *Sexologies 25,* 4, e71–e75.

12 Whittington, E. (2020) 'Rethinking consent with continuums: Sex, ethics and young people'. *Sex Education.* DOI: 10.1080/14681811.2020.1840343.

13 De Graaf *et al., Seks onder je 25e.*

14 ibid.

Chapter 7

1   De Graaf, H., Van den Borne, M., Nikkelen, S., Twisk, D. and Meijer, S. (2017) *Seks onder je 25e (Sex Under the Age of 25)*. Utrecht: Rutgers/ Soa Aids, Eburon.

2   Schalet, A.T. (2011) *Not Under My Roof: Parents, Teens and the Culture of Sex*. Chicago, IL, and London: The University of Chicago Press.

3   De Graaf et al., *Seks onder je 25e*.

4   Englander, E.K. (2019) 'Sexting in LGBT youth'. *Journal of the American Academy of Child & Adolescent Psychiatry* (Clinical Perspectives 78), *58*, 10 (supplement), S112–S113.

5   WHO (2020) *Female Genital Mutilation*. Accessed on 18/09/2021 at www. who.int/news-room/fact-sheets/detail/female-genital-mutilation

Chapter 8

1   Crone, E.A. and Dahl, R.E. (2012) 'Understanding adolescence as a period of social-affective engagement and goal flexibility'. *Nature Reviews: Neuroscience 13*, 9, 636–650. DOI: https://doi.org/10.1038/ nrn3313.

2   Siegel, D.J. (2014) *Brainstorm: The Power and Purpose of the Teenage Brain*. New York: Tarcher/Putnam US.

3   Grabovac, I., Smith, L., Yang, L., Soysal, P., Veronese, N., Turan Isik, A., Forwood, S. and Jackson, S. (2020) 'The relationship between chronic diseases and number of sexual partners: An exploratory analysis'. *BMJ Sexual and Reproductive Health 46*, 2, 100–107.

4   Rinkunas, S. (2016) *More and More Teen Girls Want to Get Plastic Surgery on Their Labia*. Accessed on 18/09/2021 at www.thecut.com/2016/04/ gynos-issue-guidelines-for-teen-labiaplasty.html

5   De Graaf, H., Van den Borne, M., Nikkelen, S., Twisk, D. and Meijer, S. (2017) *Seks onder je 25e (Sex Under the Age of 25)*. Utrecht: Rutgers/ Soa Aids, Eburon.

6   Hillman, N. (2021) *Sex and Relationships among Students Summary Report*. Higher Education Policy Institute Policy Note 30. Accessed on 18/09/2021 at www.hepi.ac.uk/wp-content/uploads/2021/04/Sex-and-Relationships-Among-Students-Summary-Report.pdf

Chapter 9

1   Frans, E. (2018) *Sensoa Flag System, Reacting to Sexually (Un)Acceptable Behaviour of Children and Young People*. Antwerpen/Apeldoorn: Sensoa/ Garant. Can be purchased at: https://shop.rutgers.nl/en/shop/themes/ sexual-education/the-sensoa-flag-system-%C2%A9/197683&page=

2   ibid.

3   ibid.

4   ibid.